P9-CEJ-081

A GRAND AFFAIR

A GRAND AFFAIR

AN ARCHITECT'S LIFELONG PASSION FOR HOTELS, SIMPLE AND SPLENDID

DAVID W. BEER

Lexington Avenue Books

NEW YORK

Printed in the United States of America

FIRST EDITION

ISBN: 978-0-692-96926-7

PUBLISHER:
Lexington Avenue Books
120 East 90th Street
New York, N.Y.
10128

Title-page photo is of the lobby of the Peninsula Hotel, Shanghai

Book design by Barbara M. Bachman

To my ever-supportive
daughter Elizabeth
and my partner Tyree Giroux,
always ready for another trip.

CONTENTS

PREFACE

THE IDEA FOR THIS BOOK CAME OUT OF A LECTURE SERIES delivered first at the Harvard Graduate School of Design and later at Cornell's Hotel School, Columbia University, and New York University. My students could not believe that I was still using a carousel packed with slides rather than some newfangled contraption controlled by a computer. Nevertheless, despite the lack of cutting-edge technology in my presentations, both students and professionals respectfully attended my talks, which took place over a period of several years. As I have done for readers of this book, after a few remarks and a smattering of history, I took the class through the actual workings of a hotel. In the spirit of "everything old is new again," as my starting point I used the venerable Ritz Hotel, London. I described how each space makes a marked impact on a guest's experience, from the entry canopy and front door, to the lobby, bar, restaurants, guest rooms and baths, the ballroom, the spa, and finally the apartments that have now become a feature of many new hotels. Pretty dry stuff. But I've tried to enliven the story with my own experiences and thoughts along with recollections of my adventures and occasional misadventures.

INTRODUCTION

GROWING UP IN NEW YORK I HAD NO reason to stay in the city's hotels. Before the New York State Thruway was built, the trip to Keene Valley in the Adirondacks on Route 9 required a night's stay in Albany at either the Ten Eyck, where Democrats stayed, or the DeWitt Clinton, where Republicans stayed. My father was one of Alger Hiss's lawyers, so you know where the Beer family broke their trip. Occasionally we stopped in Saratoga so that my parents could show me those two great hotels, the United States and the Grand Union, hotels so grand, their porches so high, and their lobbies so extensive that the memory of them still haunts me. Sadness at their demise marked the first stirring of my preservationist spirit. On occasion we stayed in motels in Lake George, an experience that might well have squelched my interest in hotels forever.

THE PALM COURT, RITZ HOTEL, LONDON.

In 1951 my aunt Ethel took my cousin, the future famous *Life* photographer John Loengard, and me on a trip to Europe, mainly to Italy. That journey kindled my lifelong passion for travel. Aunt Ethel was my father's much older sister, an independent woman who rebelled against the conventional life of my grandparents, with their town house at 51 East Seventy-Fourth Street. In 1926, much to their horror, she had traveled around the world by herself. She was only twenty-seven at the time.

Aunt Ethel certainly knew how to travel. Hardly an Auntie Mame, she shunned extravagance and fancy hotels, and instead booked us into the best second-class hotels in each city: the d'Inghilterra in Rome (now one of the city's most popular), the Berchielli on the Arno in Florence, the Metropole on the lagoon in Venice, the now defunct Oxford and Cambridge on the Faubourg in Paris, and Brown's in Mayfair in London. In Rome, Venice, and Paris I was not aware that Le Grand, The Gritti Palace, or the Plaza Athénée existed, much less, in London, the Ritz. I wonder if my aunt peered down from heaven in horror when in 1964 I began to work for the architectural firm of Welton Becket & Associates designing ultramodern hotels and checking into the Plaza Athénée as if I were to the luxe born. Probably not. She would have realized that my love of travel and hotels in general had always been more important than my newly acquired penchant for grand lobbies, even grander staircases, and glittering chandeliers.

There was a long interval between my staying at the then comparatively modest d'Inghilterra, near the end of the Via Condotti, and my checking in at the Plaza Athénée. In my day young people who lived in New York or on the East Coast flocked to

Europe on airplanes that stopped twice, first in Gander, Newfoundland, then in Shannon, Ireland; or they went steerage on small Cunard passenger ships like the *Parthia* and the *Media*. This was of course the time before jets, so the underprivileged people from the West Coast mostly had to settle for a trip to Hawaii or Mexico.

I was fresh out of college in 1956 when my parents gave me five hundred dollars for a summer in Europe. It was to last me for almost two months. I went third class on trains, which meant that between Paris and Rome I spent most of my time standing. Once I had to remain on my feet all the way to Naples, ending my journey in Taormina, Sicily.

In Paris the Hôtel Lenox and Hôtel de l'Université are still perfectly located on the Left Bank. When I first stayed in them, they cost just a few dollars a night. I have no idea how much I paid for a windowless cubicle in Damascus, my all-time least appealing guest room. That night's stay was topped only by my experience of sleeping rolled up in my raincoat on the streets of Paris. It was so late when I decided to retire that it seemed nonsensical to pay for a room. No one interfered with my surprisingly uneventful rest.

Now when I haggle with a front-desk manager for an upgrade to a suite, I bear little resemblance to the person I once was. Those endless summers of travel gave me immense opportunities to appreciate the great buildings, art, music, and culture of Europe as well as life in North Africa and the Near East. I often wonder what the history of our country would have been like if certain of our presidents, so-called leaders of the free world, had experienced similar trips as young men. Did they have enough

UNITED STATES HOTEL, SARATOGA SPRINGS, NEW YORK.

A fashionable resort spa hotel.

13079 UNITED STATES HOTEL, SARATOGA SPRINGS, N. Y.

curiosity to visit Paris and London even once? What if they'd traveled to the Near East in the early 1950s and seen, as I did, Arabs and Jews living in peace, or had the opportunity to be awed by the Persian civilization before the shah's departure from Iran? You may have heard it said that travel is broadening. Of course it is, whether you are sleeping on, as it happened in my case, the first-class deck of a ship sailing from Venice to Athens, or staying at Le Grand Hotel in Rome.

Standing in the aisles of trains, sleeping on decks, and staying in windowless rooms came to an end for me in 1964 when I joined Welton Becket & Associates and started taking business trips. Becket's firm specialized in the design of hotels. For the next twenty years I had the good fortune to indulge my love of travel with journeys to far-flung countries in Europe, Africa, and Asia in order to design hotels—most of them never built.

My first trip was to Kinshasa to work on Zaire's first international-standard hotel for the InterContinental Group. The plan was for me to share a room with another man in a hotel that rivaled my Damascus disaster in terms of seediness. Luckily, as fate would have it, I had a letter of introduction to a charming gentle-

UNITED STATES HOTEL.

The destruction of this hotel sparked my first interest in historic preservation.

man, John Mowinckel, who had worked with my father-in-law in Paris, where the latter had been American ambassador during the Eisenhower years. John had a large apartment overlooking the Congo River falls, and he invited me to stay. My time there was spent in grandeur, with a man in a cream-colored jacket hovering over me to see whether I might desire another glass of champagne. This sort of extravagance was not reflected in the final design for the InterContinental. That hotel was straightforward and pretty basic, although it eventually served as the location for Muhammad Ali and George Foreman's legendary 1974 "Rumble in the Jungle," held in the equally straightforward and basic hotel ballroom. A world-famous event, even if the setting was far from glamorous, appropriate for a boxing match perhaps, if not for a ball.

Aside from the beauty of the falls and the white-coat livery, what made the greatest impression on me in Kinshasa was, of all things, the delicious food. Many Belgian chefs had stayed on after the revolution, so the cuisine in restaurants was up to Brussels standards. What I remember most, however, are the enormous avocados, so tasty that I thought that if I ever contemplated suicide, my memory of those perfectly ripe fruits, served with a light vinaigrette dressing, would stay my hand.

More designs for InterContinental Hotels followed, including one planned for Saigon, which seemed a little odd to me considering the Vietnam War was fast approaching. Was that ballroom entrance I was designing really going to accommodate limousine traffic? An irrelevant question, I thought, given the circumstances. Never mind, I was soon traveling up the Nile, before the Aswan Dam was built, to the Winter Palace in Luxor, this time for Sheraton, enjoying the deliciously old-fashioned, unrenovated romantic splendor of that hotel, and returning on the most magnificent train trip I have ever taken. In those days the Nile was still allowed to flood the valley. Very soon the lights on our night train to Cairo failed and my dinner in a wood-paneled dining car was lit by candles as a full moon illuminated the palm trees that were reflected in the waters of the Nile. It is times like these when you realize that even if you are alone, you can have one of the most romantic experiences of your life.

I am sorry that the many hotels I designed in Egypt were never built. I had no better luck in Russia, either, where I designed hotels for Tishman Speyer in Moscow, Leningrad, and Kiev. At that time hotel service was virtually nonexistent, particularly when it came to restaurants. It wasn't until the Savoy opened around the corner from the Bolshoi Theatre that one could have a reasonable expectation of finding a roast chicken on the table in less than an hour and a half—or, indeed, at all. It was no wonder that the likes of Itzhak Perlman and Luciano Pavarotti eschewed the somewhat grander National and Metropol hotels and went to the Savoy for a square meal, something that must have been a particular priority for the late, great tenor.

In Iran we were constructing a spectacular addition to the Arya Sheraton, Shah Pahlavi's hotel. It had reached a height of seven floors when he was deposed and the job was stopped. For a time, added to the ravishing ruins visible at Persepolis were our columns and beams, exposed in downtown Tehran.

Finally, in China, one of my hotels was actually built: the Great Wall Hotel in Beijing. On the initial survey back in 1978, I was able to see a China that has since vanished, but my remem-

THE PENINSULA BANGKOK.

The hotel with its prang-like top appears as originally envisioned (left) and in its final state (right).

brance of that world was important to me when I returned in 2002 to design The Peninsula Shanghai, on the Bund. After nearly eight years, the hotel finally opened in 2009.

At this point, with more than a little fear and trepidation, I suggest hesitantly that two of my projects, had they been realized, would have been at least well known, if not iconic. The first, which I had planned for Atlantic City, made outlandish use of materials and had a striking silhouette. The other, in Bangkok for The Peninsula Hotels, would have been a distinctive and handsome landmark in a city that had a most unprepossessing skyline, but the building was brutally decapitated: Shortly before my design for Bangkok came to fruition, The Peninsula Hong Kong opened a new tower addition that sported a rooftop helicopter pad. Apparently this was a success, and now all new Peninsulas were required to have a heliport. My soaring prang-like tower was never built, and the somewhat awkward flattop construction that replaced it meant that my hopes for an understated but truly elegant hotel tower in Bangkok were dashed.

In terms of buildings actually constructed, my years of travel to those locations were not very productive. In terms of my understanding of what makes a successful hotel, the experience was invaluable. Not only did I visit extraordinary places such as those I have mentioned, but I also went to Sofia, Bucharest, Zagreb, Prague, Kiev, and Tbilisi in an era when I was often virtually the only visitor in the city. Seeing the hordes in St. Petersburg today, it's hard to imagine that once, on a White Nights evening in June, I was able to step out on the Neva in the middle of a particularly dispirited production of *Don Pasquale* at the Mariinsky Theatre without encountering a single tourist. Magical.

It was 1984 when Henry Brennan, Peter Gorman, and I, along with our new associate Mark Boekenheide, broke away from Welton Becket and started our own firm, Brennan Beer Gorman / Architects. When Julia Monk joined us we formed Brennan Beer Gorman Monk / Interiors. Our first jobs were given to us by Ron Wackrow, president and director of project coordination at ITT Sheraton Corporation, owners of the Sheraton New York, the Sheraton Manhattan, and the St. Regis. That work started us on the path to the renovation work and repositioning of hotels in New York, more than twenty in all, seven of which are nationally landmarked, as well as ones in Washington,

Boston, Philadelphia, and Hong Kong. BBG-BBGM became a major architectural design firm known for its hotel work, with offices in New York, Washington, Scottsdale, Sydney, and Hong Kong; well over 250 employees helped Peter Gorman, the super-talented architect Yann Leroy from Paris, and of course me realize our designs. I must add that before I became so specialized in designing hotels, I created many office buildings, including the old quarters of Barclays Bank on Wall Street (now ironically the Andaz Wall Street hotel), the Mellon Bank world headquarters in Pittsburgh, and more. I believe that our firm's wide range of work, including shopping complexes, department stores, and apartment towers, added to our all-around ability to design well-functioning and often imaginative hotels.

For a city so dependent on tourism, New York has a sorry history of tearing noteworthy hotels down. Since my youth, great hotels such as the Astor in Times Square, the Ritz-Carlton, and the monumental Savoy Plaza have been razed. The Mayfair Regent, the Westbury, and the Stanhope, among many others, have been converted to apartment buildings. It became BBG and BBGM's mission to renovate other hotels to make up for these conversions. This resulted in my tombstone project, the St. Regis.

Of course, there is more to hospitality design than the creation of grand hotels for the very rich. Although after the St. Regis we worked on The Plaza, The Sherry-Netherland, The Pierre, the Peninsula, and the Mandarin Oriental, we felt that it was important to design hotels that could be enjoyed by people who didn't arrive in our city via business class or private jet. We reconfigured the lobbies and some of the rooms in the New York and Boston Sheratons and the New York Hilton, leaving order and harmony where there had been chaos.

In this book, among other things, I am going to analyze each hotel space, its function, and its ability both to satisfy our needs and to give us pleasure. Virtually everyone who can afford it stays in a hotel at some point in his or her life. With any luck the experience is happy and satisfying. But we tend to check into hotels, have drinks and perhaps a meal, and sleep in our rooms without paying much attention. Many of us spend a great deal of time in hotels without the least understanding of how they work. A little knowledge will vastly increase the enjoyment of a stay, whether the accommodations are modest or grand luxe. Again, as my starting point I am using the Ritz in London—very grand indeed—to illustrate how hotels are planned and how they function. The elements that make up César Ritz's creation, from The Palm Court, the Long Gallery, and The Ritz Restaurant to its Royal Suite, have been copied and reinterpreted through the years in imaginative and wonderful ways.

I hope to provide helpful advice on how best to enjoy your stay, along with stories of my experiences, and to show why I find staying in hotels stimulating, surprising, fun, and even occasionally romantic.

A GRAND AFFAIR

CHAPTER I

A PERSONAL HISTORY OF HOTELS

THE EIGHTEENTH CENTURY WAS THE ERA when monumental churches and grandiose private palaces were built. Opera houses, theaters, libraries, and museums were really extensions of the type of architecture developed for palaces that once had been private but were now open to a rising middle class. Two types of building rapidly emerged after 1840, when rail travel became common. One was the elaborate, palatial glass-roofed railroad station terminus; the other, the hotel that graced it. A fine example of the latter was the Great Western Royal Hotel at Paddington Station in London. This was followed by others such as the St. Pancras Midland Grand Hotel, which was designed in a neo Gothic style

ST. PANCRAS HOTEL IN LONDON, 1889.

by Sir Gilbert Scott. The latter was once considered a great hotel before it fell into decline. Happily, it has now been refurbished, accommodating four hundred guests and flanked by a wonderfully renovated station boasting cheerful stores, bars, and restaurants, all very open and inviting.

I didn't stay in station hotels as they were mostly in areas that had become run-down and were a bit far from the center of the city with its cultural attractions, fine shopping, and restaurants. However, in 1953—Queen Elizabeth's coronation year—I spent the night in Glasgow on a trip with my family. We were on our way to Gleneagles, where my father and brother John would play golf before traveling on to Edinburgh. The sight of the new queen sporting her new crown as she emerged from St. Giles would be duly immortalized in my Brownie camera, the iPhone of the 1950s. The night in Glasgow was spent at the Station Hotel, in those days the city's best. Perhaps blocked out by my later sighting of the queen, I remember little about that venerable hotel except for the enormous size of my bathroom and the fluffy, properly warmed bath towel wrapped around my shoulders after my shower. I was flooded with a feeling of warmth and extravagance, a very Proustian experience in then gray, drab Glasgow.

Sumptuous hotels not connected to stations were built in various styles all over Europe and America. In 1862 the Empress Eugenie opened the eight-hundred-room Grand Hotel in Paris across from the opera house. Both buildings exhibited the splendor of the royal palaces of the previous century but were now open to the masses—or at least the affluent ones. Forty years later César Ritz opened the Ritz in London and, soon after, the Ritz in Paris, both of which set the standard for future grand palace hotels. Not to be outdone King Alfonso XIII of Spain, exhibiting national pride, built the still-marvelous Ritz in Madrid, my current favorite palace hotel, lobby, garden, and all, located next to the Prado.

Even when I was a student, hotels like the Ritz sparked my imagination and curiosity. Names like the Palace in St. Moritz, Le Negresco in Nice, and the Hôtel de Paris Monte-Carlo evoked a vision of glamour for me, while others might dream of a Notre Dame–view table at the legendary Tour d'Argent or meeting Rita Hayworth in Ciro's in Beverly Hills, although I still have a sneaker for both fantasies. Curiosity inspired action, and I was soon passing through the doors of the Plaza Athénée to have a drink in the sun-dappled, bird-chirping courtyard and even creeping upstairs to catch a view of a room while the maid was cleaning it. Fortunately, I was later able to have lunch in the garden and enjoy breakfast in my own room on a tiny balcony that had a view of the Eiffel Tower. This was a happy change from the days when I would slink upstairs and peek through the door of an elegantly decorated bedroom. Progress.

Grand hotels were built all over the world following the tradition of César Ritz, although most, if not all, were less sumptuous. Still in Europe—albeit barely—Moscow boasted the Metropol and, later, the National. In North Africa, Egypt had the Shepheard in Cairo, in Luxor the Semiramis II and the Winter Palace, and in Alexandria, the far simpler Cecil. In the Near East there was the St. Georges in Beirut and the King David in Jerusalem; in the Far East, the fabulous Taj Mahal Palace in Mumbai, Raffles Singapore, the Metropole Hanoi, the Hotel Peking, and the Peace in Shanghai (where Noël Coward wrote part of *Private*

Lives). These and many more I was able to visit in very early days before they were renovated or, in the case of Shepheard, torn down. Actually a pretty good record of preservation and a pretty good time for me to have stayed in all of them, lucky, lucky me! And in New York there is the Gotham, now the Peninsula, and of course The Plaza, which before its desecration was pretty grand, too, with its Palm Court, Oak Bar, and stately wood-paneled restaurant.

In the United States there are too many grandish hotels to mention, so I will simply name the few I worked on in New York. After Ivana and Donald Trump finished their reign as owners of The Plaza, I redecorated the rooms, removing what gold we could. I also did what I could to bring the Peninsula up to that company's incomparably high standards. I succeeded in making the hotel one of the city's most desirable destinations without gutting the building and starting again, as we did with the St. Regis.

To return to the United Kingdom for a moment, the Ritz in London was significant because it was the first hotel there to use steel-frame construction, which allowed it to rise eighteen stories over Green Park. That method of construction, common in the United States, was developed in the 1880s for office buildings, most notably in Chicago. In 1929 the seventeen-story Waldorf Astoria at Thirty-Fourth and Fifth Avenue was torn down and replaced by the Empire State Building. The grand old hotel was reborn later that year on Park Avenue as the Waldorf Astoria and Towers, an inspired masterpiece and a monument to its time and the art deco period.

In the 1930s the hotels that were built, if never as tall and inspiring, were much larger than they had been up until then. In Chicago the Palmer House has fourteen hundred rooms; the Conrad Hilton, twenty-five hundred. While the public spaces remained opulent, the guest room sizes shrank drastically. The Waldorf Astoria has some rooms as narrow as twelve feet across with tiny, three-fixture bathrooms. A more commercial hotel like the Pennsylvania opposite Penn Station has rooms as narrow as nine feet. In the case of the Waldorf, I do not wish to imply that before 2014, when a Chinese insurance company bought the hotel, our presidents stayed there in squalor. The towers wing has a separate entrance, elevators, and commodious apartments extremely suitable for our chief executive, as well as the likes of the Duke and Duchess of Windsor and Cole Porter who stayed there in days very much gone by. I sipped one of the duchess's favorite drinks, Dubonnet and gin, in the Windsors' very special suite, due to my tagging along with my in-laws Laura and Amory Houghton one evening. Being with the "D of W" as Mrs. Houghton referred to her—was amusing in its way.

After the war, when hotels with names like Sheraton, Hilton, and Marriott were being built, their designs were both similar and dull. When architect John Portman opened his first towering atrium hotel in Atlanta, soon to be followed by counterparts at Chicago's O'Hare airport, in Detroit, in San Francisco, and others, architects all over the world were inspired to open up their interiors and rethink their concepts of hotel design. Soon afterward, in 1980, with the creation of The Regent Hotel Hong Kong on the harbor opposite the venerable Peninsula, Bob Burns introduced his concept for a truly luxurious guest room. Both developments will be discussed later.

Historically there have been some hotels through the years that have come close to, and in some cases achieved, an iconic image. Certainly the great palace hotel style defined the look for luxurious properties for years. Then the art deco period dominated, from the Waldorf Astoria to dozens of examples on Miami Beach, all delightful and celebrated for their style and verve. Postwar architects, however, almost exclusively turned their talents to other types of build-

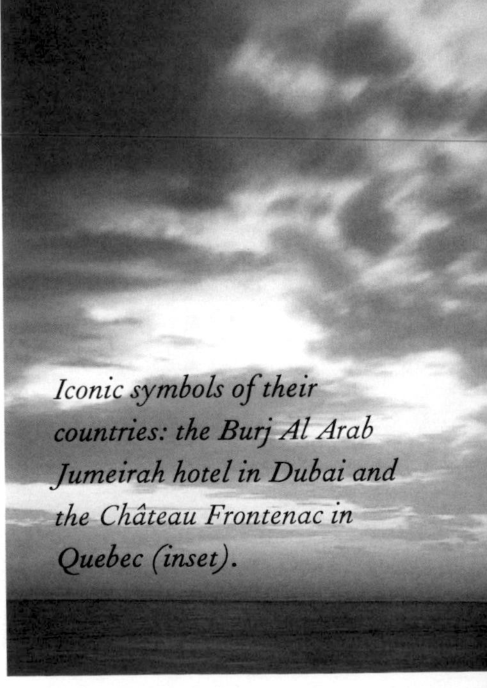

Iconic symbols of their countries: the Burj Al Arab Jumeirah hotel in Dubai and the Château Frontenac in Quebec (inset).

ing. When I was looking for a new job in 1965, there were only two firms that specialized in hotels, William Tabler and Welton Becket—and yes, of course, there was Morris Lapidus, who designed exotic fantasy resorts like the Fontainebleau and its neighbor Eden Roc in Miami Beach. These were not standard

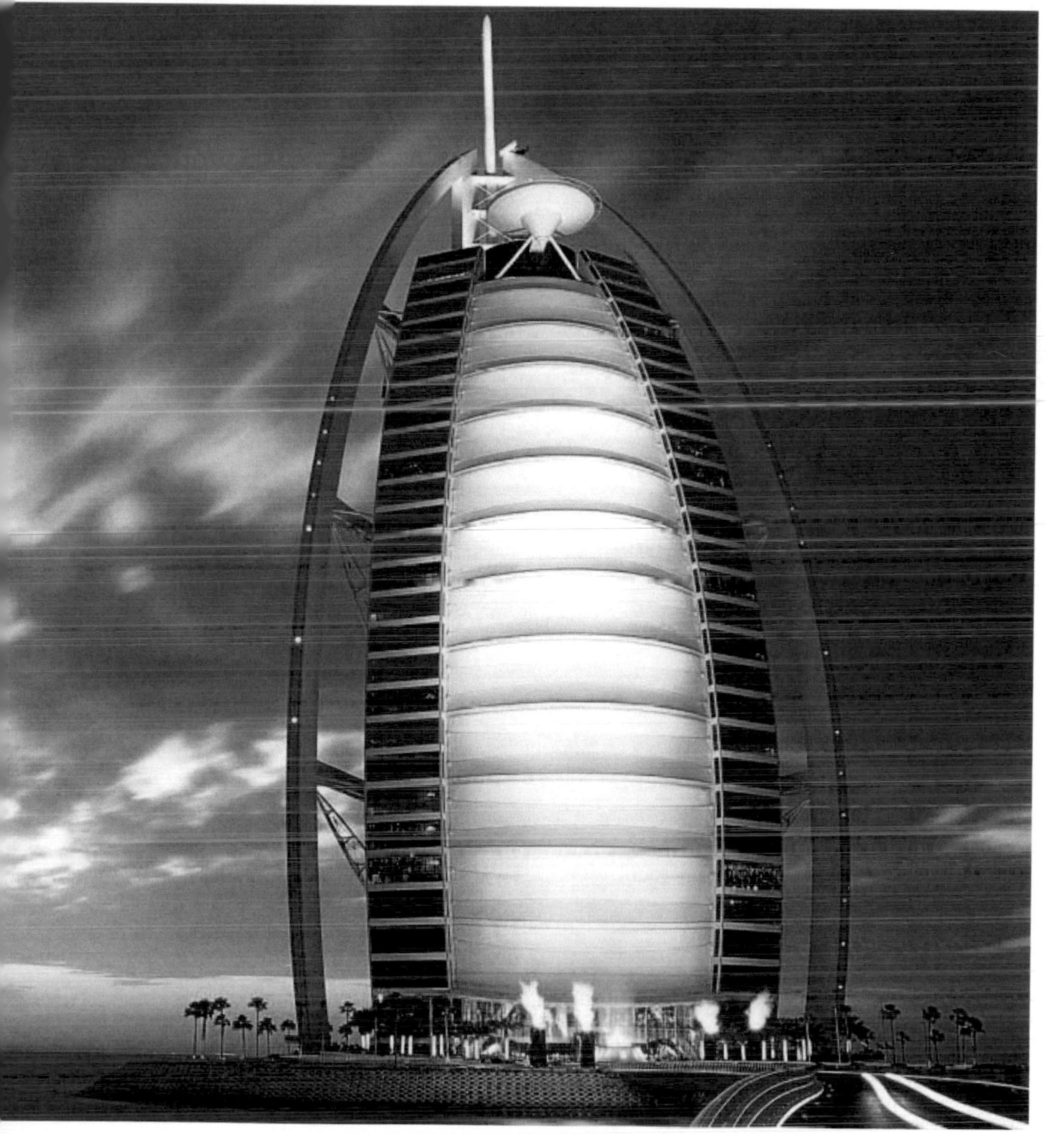

commercial hotels like Hilton and Sheraton, the kind I designed for Becket.

Perhaps the combination of Miami Beach and commercial anything contributed to the snobbery that the architectural profession as a whole attached to designing hotels. When James Stewart Polshek, then dean of the architectural school at Columbia, invited me to teach a class for a few weeks I said I would ask students to work on a hotel as a problem to be solved. "We don't do hotels at Columbia" was his reply. I am sure they do now, and in fact most successful architects are designing them—with some ravishing results such as the Aman Resorts and all those I have never visited (and I guess I never will) in Dubai. I have never attempted to travel to the roof of The Standard on the High Line for fear of an age-related rejection by the maître d', but the hotel is one of our city's most celebrated, designed by the same Jim Polshek who dismissed my proposal at Columbia in the 1960s.

The universal use of computers by designers—except me—has totally changed the shape and exterior appearance of hotels. The buildings do not look from the outside like the Ritzes of old, or even the Mandarin Orientals or most Four Seasons of today. With a computer you can now construct a tower of virtually any shape. That was fine for Frank Gehry when he was working on his extraordinary museums and theaters. It is another matter when you are planning a hotel where all the guest rooms should be nearly the same size. The Four Seasons in Hong Kong has a gently curving façade on its guest tower, designed by the vastly creative and invariably sensible architect César Pelli. Even at that hotel I am conscious of the fact that if my room is located at the end of its curve it is a few feet shorter than the ones at the center of the bulge, and for the same price of course. But in computer-generated guest room towers that twist, turn, and bulge, and not gently, room sizes can be radically different. My former client for the St. Regis, Ron Wackrow, told me when he was working for Sheraton, "The outside look of a hotel does not add one dime to the room rate." While I think this is an exaggeration, I do believe that the planning, the rooms, the public spaces, and the ambience are more important for a guest's experience than the exterior.

Many architects today start with the look of the hotel's tower without resolving problems that may be caused by the site and access to it. Nor do they give much consideration to climate, local culture, economic restrictions, height limits, and of course the client's demands. Nowadays, especially with the help of a computer, an office building can be easily shaped into almost any mass because the requirements are simpler. But as this book will illustrate, planning hotels is a vastly more complex undertaking. Even with a computer, very few of those buildings end up with an iconic silhouette. Too many practical considerations. One exception is the Burj Al Arab Jumeirah hotel in Dubai, which has become the symbol of that country, just as more than a century ago the Château Frontenac became the symbol of Quebec. The two buildings could not be less similar. I stayed in the Château Frontenac for New Year's Eve in 2000 and it worked fine. By all reports the hotel in Dubai works just fine, too. My baseball cap is off to the architect!

In contrast one of my most satisfying experiences was when I walked to the terrace of the restaurant M on the Bund in Shanghai to view the very nearly completed Peninsula hotel. For a moment I could not distinguish the contemporary tower I had designed from its landmark neoclassical and art deco neighbors, so well did it fit in. I was proud to have my tower become part of a harmonious historic ensemble rather than making a strong original statement that would have reduced the other buildings to mere background. Definitely not an iconic building, but one that was sympathetic to its surroundings and, in a word, appropriate.

For a moment I allowed myself to be proud when the head of the Shanghai commission in charge of the city's heritage told me that my name should be chiseled in stone like those of Palmer and Turner, the architects who designed a great many of the historic buildings on the Bund. Proud indeed, if just for a moment.

The author in The Peninsula Shanghai, a complex of hotel, ballrooms, shops, and apartments (below).

CHAPTER 2

FINDING THE BEST LOCATION

WHETHER YOU'RE PICKING A HOTEL for a business trip or for a holiday, a major consideration is its location. Real estate brokers are forever chanting the mantra, "Location, location, location." When it comes to your hotel, a "100 percent" location offers accessibility, convenience, and proximity to transportation, offices, shops, restaurants, and everything else that makes city life manageable and exciting.

The Ritz has London's most convenient location to be sure, sandwiched as it is between Green Park and St. James Piccadilly. It's near one of the city's snobbiest restaurants, Le Caprice, and trendiest, the Wolseley, and hard by the toniest men's clubs—White's, Brooks's, and Boodle's—along with two legendary shops,

ENTRANCE TO THE RITZ HOTEL, LONDON.

John Lobb for shoes and Lock & Co. for hats. Just down the way is Princess Diana's old place, Spencer House, and farther along Charles and Camilla's digs: St. James's Palace. Incidentally, in the middle of all this grandeur there is a pub serving steak and kidney pies and pints of bitter. And yes, there is the Underground, too, its entrance a few yards away on Piccadilly, which will whisk you to the theaters and Royal Opera House in one direction and in the other, after many stops, to Heathrow Airport. In the old days when I actually stayed at the Ritz, I spent so much money that trying to economize seemed futile, and one of those delightful black London taxis would be summoned instead of a ride planned on the Tube. Apart from the Ritz, I have probably lodged at twenty other hotels in London, from a bed-and-breakfast in Chelsea to Claridge's in Mayfair. Everyone has a favorite, but mine is now The Westbury. Located on New Bond Street, it's almost as convenient as the Ritz and certainly much more affordable. And of course for those who love the theater and are well heeled, The Savoy is traditionally the place to stay.

In Paris the perfect location is less easily defined. The Ritz commands the geographic center on the Place Vendôme, which, along with the ancient Place des Vosges in the Marais, is the city's most architecturally harmonious square. For me the area is a bit commercial, lacking as it does simple bistros and casual outdoor cafés. For formal settings and dramatic vistas, the Hôtel de Crillon on the Place de la Concorde and Le Meurice on the Rue de Rivoli are both grand beyond grand, but no one lives nearby, and Lucas Carton and Maxim's are not my idea of neighborhood restaurants.

The Four Seasons Hotel George V is on the edge of the

Golden Triangle, so named because it's bordered by three of Paris's most famous boulevards: the Avenue des Champs-Élysées, the Avenue Montaigne, and the Avenue George V. The area is crowded with both luxury and local shops and even has a few affordable restaurants. One of my favorites is Chez André, a traditional brasserie dating back to the 1930s where customers are served by elderly black-clad French women who don't speak English. Not Lucas Carton exactly.

There was a time when I always stayed at the Plaza Athénée, which is elegantly set on the tree-lined Avenue Montaigne where a select few reside in apartments above the likes of Louis Vuitton and Cartier. Marlene Dietrich lived nearby, and occasionally the reclusive star could be seen peering out of her fourth-floor window, which was almost directly across from "the Plaza"—as it was called by those in the know who lived on the Rue de Grenelle.

All the aforementioned hotels with their grand locations are, with the exception of The Westbury, very great palace hotels and incredibly expensive now. I learned many, many years ago that it was possible to find one just as well situated that cost much less.

In 1953 I was staying in Paris on the Left Bank with my brother John when somehow we learned that if we went to the American embassy we could pick up an invitation to attend the rehearsal black-tie dinner, ceremony, and reception for the wedding of American ambassador Douglas Dillon's daughter Joan to James Moseley. The fact that we didn't know them wasn't a problem. Extra men were needed, no questions asked as long as they had a tuxedo, rented of course in our case. Since the wedding took place at the magnificent Madeleine, the really rich guests stayed at the Ritz, which was almost around the corner. The others, the kind of folks my parents knew, lodged just two blocks away at the France et Choiseul, a typically charming Parisian hotel with a delightful small courtyard. It was a fraction of the cost endured by those staying at the Ritz. Today if you should want to book a room at that typically charming Parisian hotel, you may be startled to learn that it has been transformed. It is now the super-chic, super-trendy, super-expensive Hôtel Costes, and would certainly no longer appeal to my parents' friends. These days the likes of Beyoncé and Jay-Z, in town perhaps for Fashion Week, stay there.

There are many more reasons for picking a hotel other than its prestigious location on the Place Vendôme or the Avenue Montaigne. I prefer to stay near the monuments and museums I like to visit. In Paris, in order to be close by the Louvre, I choose the Hôtel Régina, or Hôtel du Louvre if I am flush; if not, the Normandy Hotel located in between. If I have a sudden urge to review French paintings or gaze at Napoléon III's apartments, I can avoid at least some of the hassle getting in by using the Rue de Rivoli entrance instead of the exposed-to-the-elements, line-plagued Pyramid entrance. In Madrid the Ritz is literally adjacent to the Prado, and it also has a splendidly opulent lobby and ravishing garden. It's a convenient choice indeed, and a hotel very well worth staying in, even at the prices.

Los Angeles's peach-pink and green Beverly Hills Hotel, famous for its Hollywood celebrities, is centrally located on Sunset Boulevard. The incident I remember most about my stay there is not an encounter with a glamorous film star, but what happened when I attempted to walk to my office at the time, Welton Becket

& Associates, which was in Century City, a couple of miles away. In those days people dressed rather formally for the office: suit, tie, the works. I was strolling on the grass, since there was no sidewalk, when a patrol car pulled up and one of the policemen inside asked me what I was doing. Apparently those officers had never seen a person walking in Beverly Hills. Perhaps Los Angeles is not a city for a non-driver like me, or Woody Allen for that matter, if either of us wishes to survive. Luckily I wasn't taken in for questioning.

In Beijing I have only one choice of hotel, the former Hotel Peking (now Raffles), an immense building in French Colonial style that was constructed in 1901. It's just a fifteen-minute walk from the entrance to the Forbidden City. I remember that walk well, and not because I was stopped by the police. Alas, only I could arrange to have my first, and fortunately teeny-weeny, stroke dead center in the middle of the Forbidden City. Luckily I was with a sturdy associate, Christian Joris, who half carried me up and down stairs to the exit on Tiananmen Square. I remember that last stretch to the hotel very well and also how quickly I recovered after a glass of Côtes du Rhône in the hotel's charming, convivial Writers Bar. Before I was stricken I had seen for perhaps the tenth time the most extraordinary complex of harmonious monumental buildings in the world. To look at it again was my reason for staying at the former Peking Raffles, which is as near as you can be and a practical choice, too, given that there are hardly any taxis to be had. Virtually none. Being within walking distance of China's most important and impressive monument is a definite and noteworthy plus.

The first question some of my friends ask me after I have

suggested a hotel is, "How is the health club?" Their most important goal is to continue their vigorous exercise regime. I want to have easy access to the Louvre. Others care most about sleeping above an Equinox. Vive la différence!

Sometimes I opt to stay in a residential area. I like the Four Seasons in Shanghai, well designed by the last firm I worked for, HOK, because it's close to the museum, the Grand Theatre, the opera house, and the center of things in People's Square. But best of all, it's a very few blocks from the French Concession, the city's well-preserved and charming old neighborhood filled with shops, restaurants, bars, and upscale apartments along streets and avenues shaded by enormous arching plane trees originally planted by the French. There are a lot fewer tourists swarming the place than you'd find on the Bund.

In New York the Carlyle Hotel on Madison Avenue and

RAFFLES BEIJING HOTEL.

Part of the original Hotel Peking, where I stayed in the 1970s.

Seventy-Sixth Street has the Metropolitan Museum, the Frick, the Jewish Museum, the Met Breuer, and Central Park. As an added asset, the hotel is surrounded by some of the Upper East Side's grandest town houses and apartment buildings. Opting to stay at the Carlyle is hardly an esoteric choice. Winston Churchill, Mrs. Onassis, and Princess Diana stayed there exclusively. Tony, certainly, but not especially convenient for business travelers.

In Jakarta a few years back, I did make an exotic choice, or at least an unconventional one, for a person doing business downtown. I decided to stay at The Dharmawangsa Jakarta, a couple of miles from the city center, in what is often referred to as the embassy area; very posh indeed, especially in contrast with drab, crowded downtown. Jakarta is another of those cities in Southeast Asia that has torn down all its glorious colonial buildings, obliterating any vestiges of its colonial past. Staying at the Dharmawangsa turned out to be very fortuitous indeed. I instantly fell in love with the cool but comfortable contemporary architecture, the spacious rooms with their high ceilings, and especially the lushly planted garden. It surrounded a remarkably inviting swimming pool, the only one I have ever seen that had an arch of trees extending from both sides completely shading the pool below. And yes, there were a few cheerful pool boys to catch the inevitable floating leaves. Adding to this idyllic suburban experience, I received a call from Kartika, President Sukarno's daughter, inviting me to have dinner with friends, many friends as it turned out, at a restaurant around the corner. Although Indonesia is the world's largest Muslim country, you certainly wouldn't have guessed it from the crowd there, fashionably dressed with nary a burka nor even a head scarf in sight, although there were a few

Hermès scarves draped decoratively around the ladies' shoulders. I could have easily imagined myself in the back room on the Upper East Side at Swifty's, which was the favorite of a similar crowd. Sadly, it's now closed and sorely missed by its habitués, among them probably Kartika when she is in town from London, where she now lives.

THE PENINSULA

CHAPTER 3

ENTRANCES AND CANOPIES

MGM'S STAR-STUDDED MOVIE *GRAND Hotel* defined my expectation of what such a luxury establishment must have been like in the 1930s. Since the story is set in Berlin, I had always assumed that the dazzling sets were based on the Adlon, which was the city's most celebrated hotel. In fact that building, with its art deco touches, was very restrained and conventional in comparison with the towering structure created for the film. The film hotel was built around a gleaming multistory circular atrium made of metal and glass. The other thing that impressed me in the film was that those "people come people go" through a gigantic revolving door. It always looked as if the next couple might at any time be Fred and Ginger, he in tails, she in shimmering white chiffon under an ermine coat.

ENTRANCE TO THE PENINSULA SHANGHAI.

This vision was a far cry from the actual experience of arriving at The Ritz London. It would be difficult to ascend so gracefully that hotel's steep stairs, which begin quite far from the sloping curb of St. James's Street.

Whether you arrive at your hotel by foot or taxi, the canopy is the first thing you see. The one that shields the entrance to the Ritz in London is very small, a decorative, semicircular metal and glass affair set rather high above the stairs leading from St. James's Street to the front doors. Given London's famously inclement weather, it's surprising that the Ritz canopy isn't large enough to shield arriving guests entirely from the rain. Even though it is now augmented by a second one made of blue canvas, the canopy is still inadequate as a protection against those London downpours. Perhaps the entrance to that undeniably grand hotel is not the grandest, but a helpful doorman in a morning coat, his gray top hat decorated with a black band, will meet you at the curb with a large umbrella, unless he is helping another party out of a taxi. Of course the hotel has regular traditional doors. It's hard to imagine the presumably fastidious César Ritz revolving in any way.

Virtually all hotels are planned these days with very broad canopies, so an umbrella is rarely needed from taxi to front door. A few hotels even have regular doors, which I always thought were de rigueur for grandness until I saw *Grand Hotel*.

More typically, hotels from the Peninsula to the Marriott have very large canopies that cover at least the first car lane, except in New York where no structure is allowed to extend over the curb. In Las Vegas the canopies are gargantuan, big enough to shelter many cars and even a few tour buses. They generally

WALDORF ASTORIA HOTEL, NEW YORK.
The entrance canopy was designed when I was at HOK.

have skylights so guests don't feel as though they are entering a tomb-like underground parking garage. That would hardly be the appropriate introduction to one of those gloriously glitzy lobbies just beyond the front door.

On the other hand, the Luxor in Las Vegas might actually profit from a tomb-like entrance, since the interior of that pyra-

THE PENINSULA BANGKOK.

A warm greeting at the door is always welcome.

mid-like structure has an ancient pyramid tomb theme—and very dark and gloomy it is.

I have to admit I do like having doors opened for me at hotels when I am carrying packages (a rare occurrence) or when I am wheeling my suitcase to the entrance. At this stage in my life I appreciate all the help I can get. I used to think that grand hotels eschewed revolving doors, until I visited Vienna last year and discovered that the Imperial, the Bristol, and even the revered, classic Hotel Sacher have them. I have gone through them many times on my way to have a drink at the bar or a memorable meal at the Café Rouge.

Revolving doors are almost universal now, eliminating the need for a second pair beyond the vestibule to guard against cold air seeping into the lobby. These doors are used in today's most deluxe hotels as well as others. However, if you happen to arrive at a hotel that has a huge circular contraption, always automatic and usually with those fake flowers floating in the middle, you are probably not entering one of those establishments that in the Michelin Guide boasts a full complement of turrets, some colored black, or better still red, signifying they are grand luxe.

My favorite entrance doors are those of the Peninsulas in Hong Kong, Bangkok, and Shanghai, where two ever-smiling boys in white uniforms and jaunty hats open both sides as you enter past two white porcelain lions, one male, and one female nursing her cub. The lions are, in fact, an almost universal adornment to entrances in Chinese hotels. You know you are not walking into a Holiday Inn in Sandusky, Ohio.

CHAPTER 4

GRAND (AND MODEST) LOBBIES

THE FRONT DESK IS LOCATED EITHER JUST before the main lobby or right in it. The Ritz in London has a small, elegant lobby that contains only the front desk and a relatively modest grand staircase. Bills are settled in a small room discreetly out of sight.

In today's world this lobby is most probably unique, because a man in a morning coat guards its double doors, ensuring that all men who venture in are wearing a jacket and tie. Old World indeed! If they are "properly attired," guests may walk down a long promenade flanked by sofas and chairs, which leads first to The Palm Court and then, at the end, to The Ritz Restaurant. The promenade is called descriptively if

LOBBY OF THE WALDORF ASTORIA, NEW YORK.

rather plainly the Long Gallery. Similar spaces were created at The Royal Hawaiian in Honolulu and more recently at the Royalton in New York, the latter the place to be seen if you were in the fashion industry in the 1980s. To be seen, yes, but probably not in a jacket and tie.

The lobby at the Ritz is modest compared with those of many great palace hotels, and certainly with today's atrium extravaganzas. But discreet, modest lobbies exist in some of the world's most prized and prestigious hotels, such as The Ritz Paris, the Carlyle and The Lowell in New York, and the Huntington in San Francisco. Despite all Donald Trump's bellicose self-aggrandizement, the Trump International at Columbus Circle has a surprisingly modest lobby. Definitely not *HUGE.*

Lobbies modest or grand still boast an actual physical front desk, although some in the industry foresee the day when all checking in will be done electronically. This will obviously not suit me, fussy as I am with my predilection for seldom accepting the first or the even second room that is shown to me. Nevermore will the guest have physical key in hand, even the plastic kind, and certainly never again one of those metal ones with braided streamers attached, once so common in grand hotels. And for me, no more cheery greetings of "Welcome back, Mr. Beer."

Personally, I like the practice common in many hotels of requiring you to put your key in the lock before you can turn on the light in your room. This saves energy, of course, but for me it means I know where I have left my key, and will avoid the frantic search when a phone call tells me my taxi has arrived.

The St. Regis, which opened in 1905 on Fifth Avenue, also has a small lobby. When we were asked to renovate it in 1986, we discovered that it was originally a two-story space giving onto Fifth Avenue that had been converted to stores. This may have been a sensible economic decision, but it left the hotel without a grand living area. Our solution was to move the King Cole Bar as far as possible to the eastern side, which would open up to a newly created two-story atrium. This space, which today's guests assume has always been there, is appropriately named Astor Court after the hotel's developer John Jacob Astor. Incidentally, except for that small check-in lobby, half of the second-floor function rooms, the Versailles Room, all the hotel's other rooms, and even the roof were taken back to concrete, completely reconfigured and redesigned. When I accompanied Mrs. Vincent Astor on a tour of the renovations she exclaimed, "It is just as I remember it when Vincent and I lived here." Not so.

After the First World War, Prohibition, and the Depression, hotels were built with much more modest guest rooms. Probably to compensate for this, in the 1930s their lobbies were often very grand. Some that we have worked on include the Palmer House in Chicago, the Shoreham in Washington, and the Palace and the Waldorf Astoria in New York. The Waldorf was built in 1931 and has one of the greatest art deco hotel lobbies in the world. HOK vastly improved it by creating a three-story-high lobby at the Park Avenue entrance, which had formerly been divided into three separate stories. This innovation was the idea of our collaborators, the immensely talented designers Alexandra Champalimaud and, from our office, Greg Cranford, who created the elegant metal and glass canopy on Park Avenue.

If you climb the Waldorf's stairs you can stroll all the way to Lexington Avenue while enjoying the hotel's successions of

ATLANTA MARRIOTT MARQUIS.
One of John Portman's soaring lobbies.

spaces. The experience reminds me what it was like to promenade on the great ocean liners such as the *Queen Mary*, *Queen Elizabeth*, and *Normandie*, grand floating palaces also built in the 1930s. I was lucky enough to have traveled on the *Queen Elizabeth* with my parents, cabin class of course, although my brother and I spent most of our time in first class pursuing the daughters of more affluent parents. Those great ships are part of a lost world, a distant but cherished memory. An even dimmer memory for me is of the times I spent in Atlantic City cruising the fabulous fantasy hotels that still existed there in the 1950s. What a pity that the extravagant lobbies of gargantuan establishments like the Traymore and the Marlborough-Blenheim were not preserved and integrated into the new hotels that were built in their place, which attempted to re-create the fantasy and failed miserably.

In 1967 architect-developer John Portman created a new kind of fantasy lobby when he designed an atrium for the Hyatt Regency Atlanta. It was to revolutionize the look of many modern hotels. The lobby extends from the ground all the way to the top of the last guest room floor. He also developed this

concept in Chicago, San Francisco, New York, Detroit, and other cities. When I was asked to design the first thousand-room convention hotel in the Far East, the Great Wall Sheraton in Beijing, it was mandatory that I include a multistory atrium lobby. The

Chinese wanted a modern American hotel, and this meant an atrium. An atrium they got, and for years that hotel, with its many restaurants, meeting rooms, and grand ballroom, was the social and diplomatic center of Beijing. No one seemed to care that the mirror-glass windows on the outside had been installed backward so they reflected into the rooms—whose occupants were plainly visible on the outside—spoiling what was to be a mono-

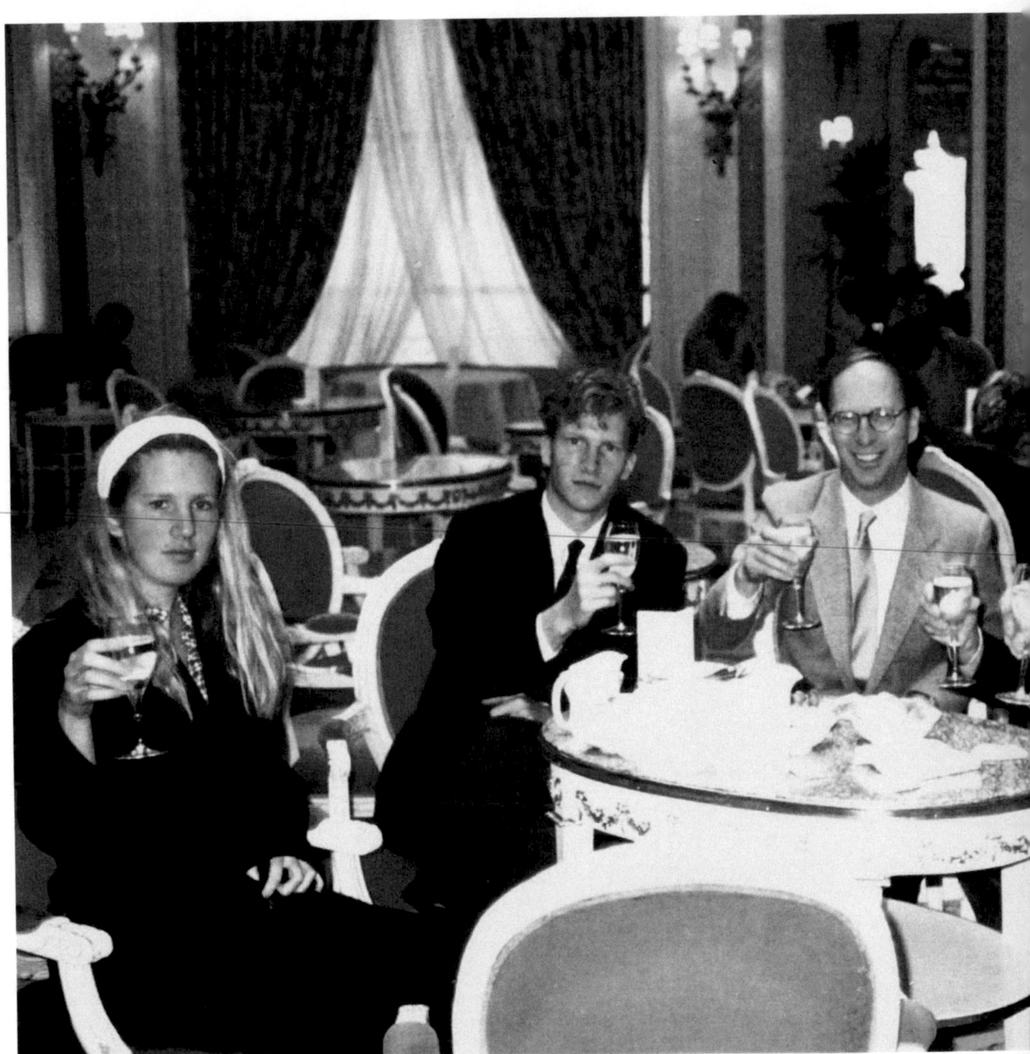

chromatic reflective façade. When the architect of the Taj Mahal Palace in Mumbai discovered that his building had also been constructed backward, he committed suicide. Clearly, I did not.

The idea of the central glass-covered lobby was partly an outgrowth of the skylight palm courts at the Ritz in London, the Palace in Madrid, and the Palace in San Francisco. The Palm Court at the Ritz is one of the world's most elegant spaces architecturally. It's now so popular that tea there begins as early as twelve o'clock and continues well into the evening. I must confess that even though men do wear the required ties and jackets, the crowd does not quite live up to the surroundings. Happily everyone seems to be having a wonderful time. The Palm Court wasn't as popular in the days when my family and I would come to London. We never missed a chance to meet there on at least a few late mornings for champagne—not tea—before having a glorious lunch in The Ritz Restaurant down the way. This is where I would treat my goddaughter Emily Fletcher after I had fulfilled my godfa-

THE RITZ HOTEL, LONDON.
Properly dressed for Ma's birthday, the Beer family drinks champagne in The Palm Court.

therly duty and taken her to the nearby St. James's Piccadilly to hear the charismatic Reverend Donald Reeves denounce Margaret Thatcher in one of his powerful, thought-provoking sermons. The Palm Court is where, with my children Elizabeth and Andrew, we celebrated my mother's seventieth birthday, a cliff-hanger as it turned out. When we met at JFK both children had forgotten their passports. They had to fly over the next day, getting to London just in time for our drinks at the Ritz. Kids.

It's a long way from the Ritz's Palm Court to Portman's atrium hotels, and even farther to the almost sixty-story lobby Skidmore, Owings & Merrill designed for the Shanghai Grand Hyatt in dreaded Pudong. Years ago now, I took a group from the Knickerbocker Club in New York on a trip to the city and escorted them to the roof of that

THE PENINSULA HONG KONG. *The lobby is the place to meet in HK.*

hotel. When we arrived at the top, many of us could not bear to look down and clung to the wall as far away from the railing as we could get. Extravagant and breathtaking the view may have been, but terror and vertigo are not the emotions you want to experience on your way to a bar, any bar. Shock and awe on the road to a martini. In Jakarta and Hong Kong, fortunately, Hyatt

has developed hotel lobbies that are less impressive but more scaled to humans. More like four stories, each has a grand stairway that allows a bride to make an impressive entrance on her way to the grand ballroom.

The Peninsula Hong Kong is more in the European tradition. I discovered the hotel when I visited China for the first time in the 1970s, hoping to find inspiration for my designs for the Great Wall Hotel, which soon became a Sheraton. It was simple living in Beijing in those days—not even one skyscraper had yet been built, and the traffic consisted mostly of bicycles. Although I enjoyed the city, which was still remarkably picturesque, I had a problem with meals. My boss at the time, MacDonald Becket, refused to eat Chinese food because he had a seafood allergy. We were doomed to take every meal in a restaurant, its dining room overlit day and night, where he was able to find the only food he could tolerate: Marco Polo's discovery, spaghetti. After that culinary non-adventure I went to Hong Kong, where I stayed at the Sheraton in Kowloon. From my bedroom window I could see the spectacular harbor and the palatial Peninsula. Once I'd paid a visit to that hotel and seen its white marble lobby, I only returned to the Sheraton to sleep.

Years later we designed a new bar and a restaurant called The Verandah, as well as remodeling the Peninsula's fancy haute cuisine restaurant Gaddi's, which proudly proclaimed that it served "the best French food east of Suez." In those days I spent much of my time in The Lobby, then and now an absolutely gorgeous, bustling, music-filled space. The Peninsula is owned by the Hong Kong and Shanghai Hotels company, whose concept was to create a grand lobby at the entrance to the building. This space acts as a sort of town center and a place to meet between trips to peruse the dozens of high-end boutiques that adjoin it.

Breakfast, lunch, tea, drinks, and dinner are served in The Lobby all day and evening. I believe one of the reasons it attracts so many people is that it's a gracious, Old World oasis away from the decidedly seedy activities outside in Kowloon. A trip across Nathan Road is always an exercise in denials. No, I do not want a Rolex, no, I do not want a Vuitton bag, no, I do not want to sleep with you, miss, no, mister, I do not want to sleep with you, either. No wonder locals refer to Kowloon as "the dark side." It was very different when the Kadoorie family built the hotel in 1928, and even when I visited in 1978, half a century later.

In the years that followed, we designed several hotels for Peninsula, three of which were actually finished: the renovation of The Peninsula New York and their hotels in Bangkok and Shanghai. I was guided on all three projects by their design director John Miller, who brilliantly shepherded my work from my first conceptual sketches to the final choice of materials.

The Lobby in The Peninsula Shanghai echoes the one in Hong Kong and has a similar grand space right at the front door. I have received some criticism from friends for this design. But these critics don't know that such grand lobbies right at the entrance are a Peninsula standard and not to be questioned in any way unless the designer wishes to invoke the wrath of all concerned, including the chairman. I learned from years of experience that there are some edicts of the otherwise surprisingly flexible Sir Michael Kadoorie that one does not question. The Lobby in the hotel in Shanghai is particularly successful, tall with strong, soaring columns on each side leading to windows that

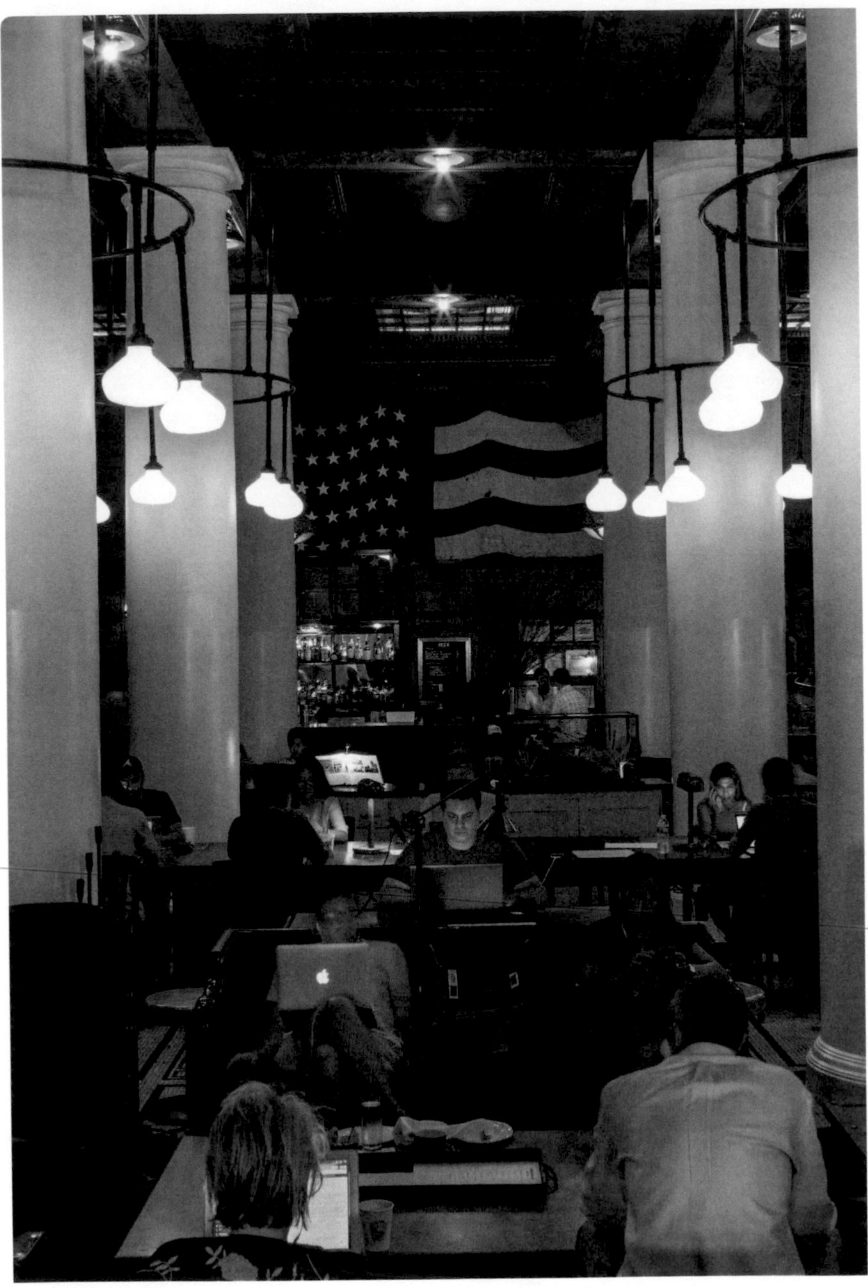

THE ACE HOTEL NEW YORK.

The place for millennials to meet in NYC.

look into the garden and trees of the former British consulate. I laid out and planned all the spaces, which were brilliantly decorated by the Parisian Pierre-Yves Rochon. This Lobby is a worthy successor to its world-famous counterpart in Hong Kong thanks in large part to his creative design work.

Lobbies have always been places where you can relax, have a cup of tea or a drink, and settle into a comfortable pillow-covered sofa or a heavy, difficult-to-move armchair. But they are also places to socialize, meet the locals, and catch up on news. For a while now they have been even more meet-and-greet, thanks to an idea pioneered by Barry Sternlicht, chairman of Starwood Hotels & Resorts and creator of the highly successful W Hotels. He replaced the hushed, rigid seating groups normally found in hotel lobbies with light, less plush, but easily movable chairs, many of them set around long wooden tables where people can put their computers or consult their cellphones. The hottest lobby in New York is in the Ace Hotel on Twenty-Ninth Street just off Fifth Avenue. As hotelier Andrew Jeffries has commented, "The Ace has a great combination of hotel guests and locals from the neighborhood in its public spaces. Hotels like the Carlyle and Claridge's have always had the perfect mix of people in their lobbies. And Ian Schrager's hotels, too. You sense it as soon as you walk in. It adds a feeling of authenticity and belonging." That said, the Ace Hotel is a far cry from the quiet elegance of the lobby at the London Ritz.

CHAPTER 5

STAIRCASES

More than One Way to Descend

FROM THE DISCREET STAIRCASE IN THE CORner of the modest lobby of the Ritz in London to the flamboyant, bride-displaying grand versions found in Asian hotels, staircases often form the main decorative element of a hotel lobby. Dramatic views and level changes were part of the excitement created in palaces like Versailles, Schönbrunn, and the Hermitage, so when designers created the great palace hotels, they naturally took their inspiration from these monumental buildings. The grand staircase in Vienna's Hotel Imperial is hardly distinguishable from the ones in palaces nearby—not surprising, since the hotel was originally a private palace, too. Simpler but no less dramatic creations over

THE PENINSULA SHANGHAI.

W UNION SQUARE, NEW YORK.

David Rockwell's interiors add drama to BBG's architecture.

the years have included the metal and glass staircases in station hotels such as St. Pancras in London, which may have inspired the decorative metal staircase in the Soho Grand.

In the twentieth century, the importance of the grand staircase was perhaps best exemplified by the dramatic, sweeping version designed by Morris Lapidus for the Fontainebleau Miami Beach. The stair was actually a complete fake; it went nowhere. At The Peninsula Shanghai we designed a very grand staircase that was visible from the reception lobby. It's not to be compared to the fake stair in Miami, but it does suggest that it leads to a grand ballroom and not merely to a handful of small meeting rooms on the second floor. David Beer met Morris Lapidus at least this once, and only once.

I was more than pleased when David Rockwell created a dramatic staircase for the lobby of the W Union Square. BBG was the architect and I was the designer for the project. It transformed the landmarked Guardian Life Building into what was then the most profitable W, Starwood's fresh and trendy youth-oriented brand, which was a worldwide success. As a designer, I am most closely identified with more traditional hotels, not surprisingly because of my work on projects like the St. Regis, the Peninsula, and the Pierre. To me, all projects present problems to be solved, whether the style is to be Louis XV or contemporary. I try to create designs that won't look dated in a few years. Timeless. The W and its staircase exemplify this philosophy.

For years I marveled at pictures of the most impressive hotel grand staircase ever conceived, the one at the Hotel Imperial Vienna. But when I finally saw it last year I was surprised to discover that a matching staircase anticipated for the other side had never been constructed. I was even more surprised that this grand staircase had no handrail, not even a small projected molding. As I cannot use a staircase without a handrail anymore, I was deprived of the experience of ascending to what I assume must be splendid spaces on the floor above. Since the Imperial was built before the invention of the elevator I wondered how elderly Habsburg royals reached the floor above in one piece without anything to grab on to. Maybe they used the back servants' staircase, allowing this, one of the grandest palaces on the Ringstrasse, to be deemed handicapped-accessible.

When I'm staying in a hotel, before going downstairs I often put on a jacket and occasionally even a tie, knowing full well that I will be unashamedly dressed like my father, if not my grandfather who wore spats. Maybe it's a matter of habit, for I remember a time when such behavior would have been considered de rigueur. I still think staying in a hotel can be romantic, and that a sense of ceremony is in order. When I'm alone I do not merely go downstairs; I descend. *Descend* is a pretentious word and yet it describes perfectly the act of walking deliberately down a staircase, anticipating the lights, the glow, and the crowds of people in the lobby. I savor the moment. I don't hurry toward the lobbies of the Plaza Athénée, Le Grand in Rome, and the Hôtel du Palais in Biarritz. I am alone. I am feeling good, perhaps even looking good, and I might meet someone in the bar, but probably not. It doesn't matter, because to me on those grand staircases I am ex-

HOTEL IMPERIAL VIENNA.

Dramatic, but no handrail to assist my ascent.

periencing the magic of staying in a great hotel. Of all my memories, the one I treasure most is descending the staircase at the Shah Abbas in Isfahan. Again, I had actually dressed, or at least worn a jacket, for lunch, which is hard to believe since most of the other guests were in shorts. But I was savoring the moment of being by myself, slowly proceeding toward the exotically decorated dining room of the most famous, the most sought-after hotel in Persia, a very grand staircase experience in a very grand, grand hotel.

SHAH ABBAS, ISFAHAN, IRAN.

Dramatic, and with a handrail that aided me as a guest in 1978.

CHAPTER 6

GUEST ROOMS

A Home Away from Home

SOME OF MY FRIENDS CLAIM THAT THEY don't care how appealing their guest room is; "I only go to hotels in order to sleep." Others, even if they own eleven-room apartments on Fifth Avenue and houses in Southampton and Palm Beach, prefer to stay with friends when they are traveling. For them a hotel is an unnecessary extravagance. I find this astonishing. I love staying in hotels. Camping out with friends and having to participate in their daily routine is my idea of hell.

No matter how little time I may end up spending in my guest room, I care very much about its comfort and quality. When I travel with my trusty partner Tyree Giroux, he knows to find a chair in the lobby and relax while I go up-

THE PENINSULA HOTEL SHANGHAI.

stairs with some hapless front-desk employee to make sure that the room will be the best available, as I soundly reject candidates for some seemingly obscure reason or other.

Just as a good location is important when you're choosing a hotel, so is the location of your room. Be wary about asking for one on an upper floor if you're booking into a grand palace hotel. Ceiling heights diminish in these buildings the farther up the

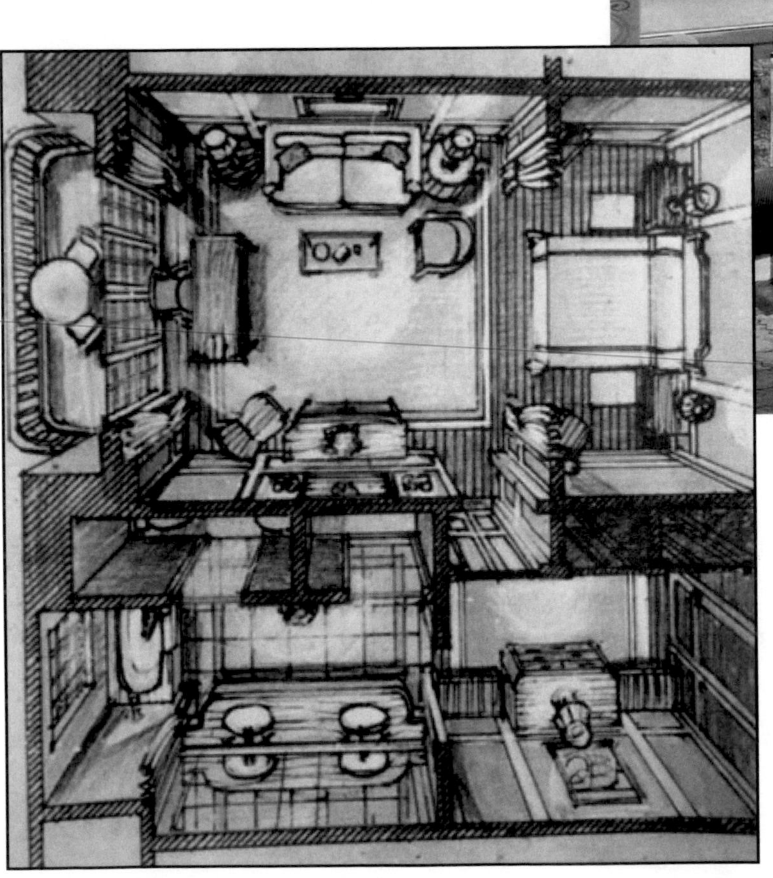

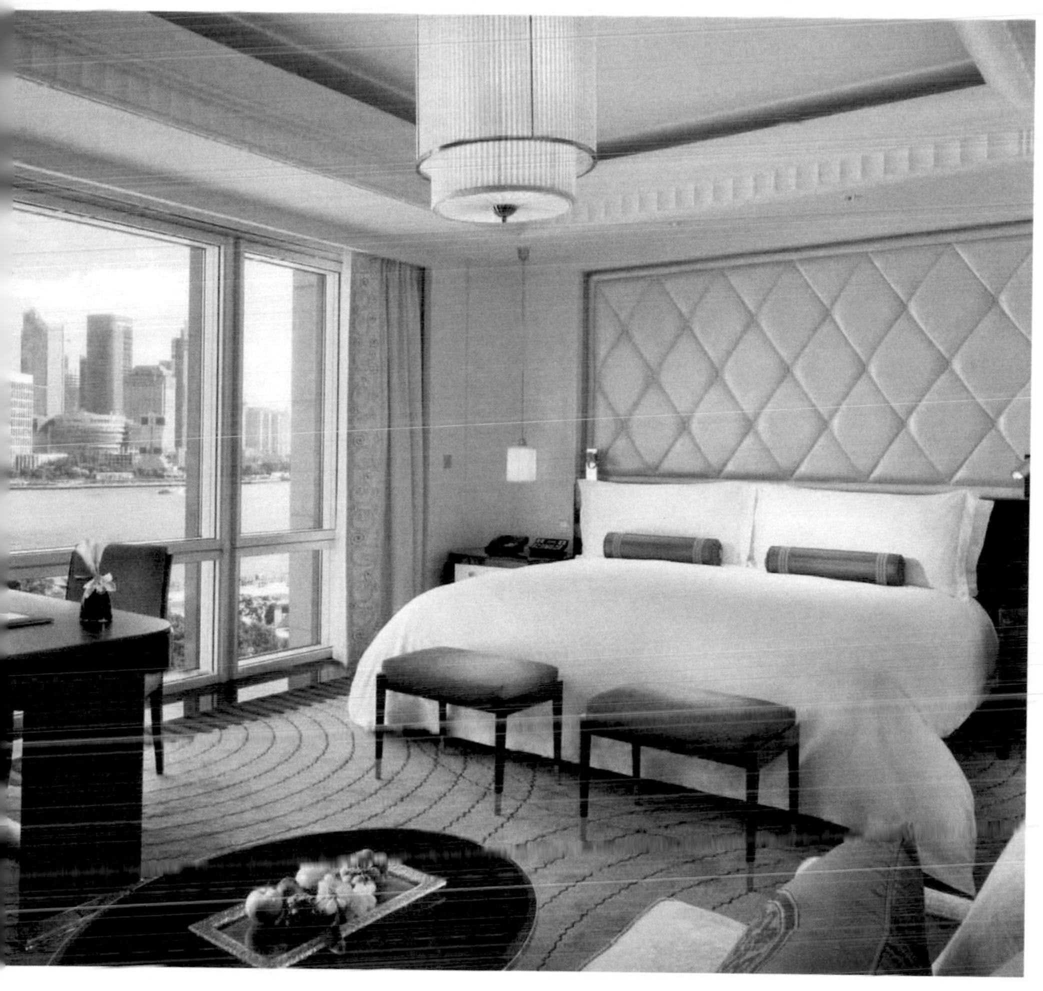

THE PENINSULA SHANGHAI.
A typical luxurious guest room (above) and one I imagined (inset).

room is located. The highest ceilings are on the second floor (in Europe called the first floor). The great royal or imperial suites are located just above the lobby floor, their lofty ceilings all the better for displaying glittering chandeliers. But all grand palace hotels have reasonably large rooms—except for those originally built for servants. They are tucked away on the top floor in the mansard roof and have tiny windows. Now many of those have been redesigned and are advertised as "loft rooms." The windows are still tiny. Gary Cooper's spacious suite in *Love in the Afternoon*, which once belonged to Coco Chanel and was decorated by her, is located on the second floor of the Ritz, just above the hotel's entrance on the Place Vendôme.

In general, I see little advantage to having a room near the top. In the morning you have to wait as the elevator stops for guests below. As for the view, it's usually just as good from the lower floors.

At a modern hotel, if you want or are upgraded to a club room you will find yourself on one of the top floors. Staying fifty, sixty, seventy floors up does not appeal to me. For a start, you don't necessarily get the best view from there. To give one example: From a high vantage point inside the Park Hyatt Shanghai—which is in charmless Pudong—you will have a view of the entire city, not of the historic Bund waterfront that lies far, far below. In New York the best views of Central Park aren't from the top, but from the sixth to twelfth floors of the Mandarin Oriental, Essex House, and, yes, Trump International.

More important than the size of your room is, of course, how it's planned and decorated, although if you don't like the way it looks, rest assured that it will soon be changed. The upholstery, curtains, and rugs are redesigned every six or seven years, and not always with the most attractive results. Unfortunately sometimes when you return a few years later, your once appealing room will have lost its charm.

Even though I prefer large accommodations, one of my hap-

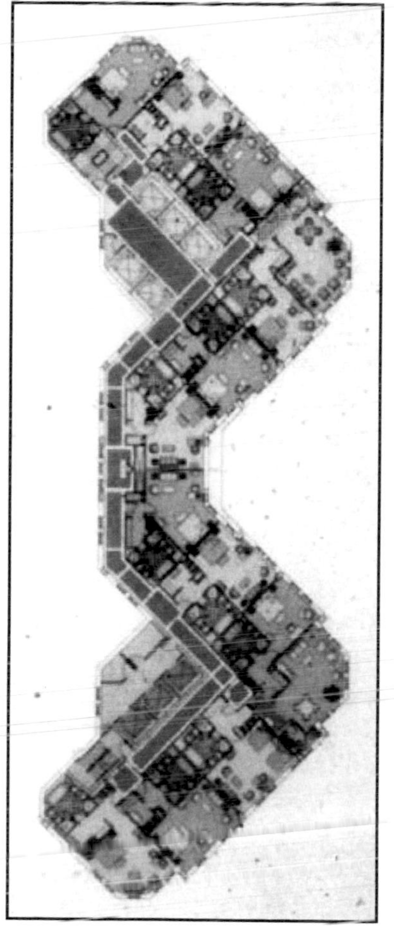

THE PENINSULA BANGKOK.
All rooms have river views.

piest times was spent in a small but exquisitely designed chamber in the elegant Vier Jahreszeiten in Hamburg. It is the only time I have ever slept in a canopy bed. It was flat against the wall, and I loved having that canopy hovering over my pillow.

If your hotel is by the sea, near a mountain range, or on a historic city square, obviously you'll want a room with a view. Getting one is not guaranteed. If you are not given the glorious advertised panorama, your room will probably be euphemistically labeled as having a "city" or "garden" view—which may even include a peek at the parking lot or, worse yet, the service entrance. Regrettably those great view symbols in the red Michelin Guides do not apply to all rooms. Beware.

I have spent a lifetime fighting to secure a room with a view, whether it was the charming corner one in the Grand Hotel in Florence that looks both across the Arno River and farther east to the Ponte Vecchio, or the one at the Hotel Nassauer Hof in

Wiesbaden that overlooks the colonnades of the magnificent Kurhaus, the eighteenth-century casino where Dostoyevsky gambled so passionately.

Nevertheless, sometimes I wonder why I fight so hard for such great rooms. Unless mine has a balcony, I often take a quick look out the window—and once I'm satisfied I have best view, I pay little attention to it again. Such a room, of course, is considerably more expensive, and in the new reality of my life I often ask for a quiet one instead. This I did at the venerable Shangri-La Hotel in Hangzhou, which has an amazing vista of West Lake and the hills and pagoda beyond. But I didn't miss it: All of it could be seen perfectly from the room serving breakfast and drinks just down the hall.

When I do acquire a room with a view, I only really appreciate it if I have a balcony. Sadly, The Regent Hotel Hong Kong, now the InterContinental, doesn't have any balconies at all, despite the fact that it has one of the most spectacular views in the world, across the harbor to the towers beyond.

I love to have breakfast on a balcony (in my case, dining on the complimentary fruit and cookies sent to me by the management; I'm too cheap to order from room service). I like to sit out there with a drink from the minibar before dinner, too, and certainly with a nightcap in hand before going to bed. A full moon is always a bonus. One of my fondest memories is the final beer of the night (not perhaps the best idea after a wine-filled dinner with Tyree) taken on a moonlit balcony facing the Aegean Sea at the Apollon Suites Hotel in Evia, Greece. On another occasion, in even grander circumstances, we had a late-night glass of wine on my balcony at the Mandarin Oriental, Sanya, facing the South

China Sea. Both those hotels have single-loaded guest room towers, and all their rooms face the sea. My old firm's clients who are developing resorts in China nowadays insist that all their rooms have views. This is easily done on a small property, less so in a hotel that has twelve hundred rooms. I tried.

The developer Robert Burns was the first to create the compartmentalized bathroom, now to be found in virtually all five-star hotels around the world. He did this for the Regent in Hong Kong with Skidmore, Owings & Merrill. His bathroom was designed with two sinks, an oversized tub, a WC in an enclosed space, and a stall shower. A new standard had been set. Burns invented the modern deluxe bathroom, and his work inspired further inventiveness from designers who came after him. One variation, created by Sir Michael Kadoorie for his Peninsula hotels, has two separate sinks on facing walls. No sharing of counter space for toothbrush and moisturizer allowed in his hotels.

Like most people, I take showers. I have not taken a bath in years. I understand that bathtubs are essential for children, and I'm sure some women prefer them to conserve the artistry of their favorite hairdresser. Bathtubs have their uses, but for most of us they are superfluous. With this in mind, I wonder why so much is being made of the tub, which now occupies the star position in many of the latest guest rooms. It has been uprooted and given a prime spot in the living area, right in front of the window, flaunting its existence. This bathtub, moreover, is invariably six feet long. Most of us can't reach our feet all the way to the end so when we get in, we find ourselves slowly slipping down into the water. Only a six-foot-six Texan can gain a foothold. But no such manly-man, I think, would be caught dead in a bathtub.

When Tyree and I were in Hong Kong in the early 1990s staying at The Landmark Mandarin Oriental (not to be confused with the legendry Mandarin Oriental just around the corner, where many of the rooms do have dramatic views), we were surprised to find that a six-by-six-foot round virtual swimming pool took up the space between the window and our beds. What view there was, we had across an empty sea of white porcelain. The Edition, Ian Schrager's boutique hotel in Miami Beach, has the right idea. No bathtubs at all, only showers.

On a more serious note, I find the placement of showers with swinging glass doors on high bathtubs dangerous, particularly for the elderly. As a rule there is nothing for a person to grab on to. In 2016 the Palace in Madrid renovated all their guest rooms, installing this arrangement. When I told the front desk that I couldn't manage the shower safely, they were forced to give me a suite because they couldn't find another room with a stall shower. I settled in happily until I became aware that a large treadmill was blocking my view out the window. I found it an unwelcome reminder that I was not keeping up with my gym activities, so I asked for it to be removed. My pleas were unanswered. Next time, back to the Ritz across the way, which has stall showers in every room as well as bathtubs, and outdoors, that ravishing garden.

My thoughts on hotel bathrooms would not be complete without a brief discussion of toilets. I prefer simple ones, not those all tricked up with heated seats and mysterious jets and sprays. I like using handles for flushing, preferably located on the right side because I am right-handed, in my mind a reassuring sign of normalcy. Flushing a toilet is one of the things I do not need help with, and those automatic seeing-eye devices occasionally neglect to see me. A slight I can do without.

Before the war my family lived in the West Village, which in those days was still pretty Bohemian. In keeping with the style of the neighborhood I was sent to a progressive school that still exists called City and Country. I was a wiz at blocks but I never learned to read, not a word. The school didn't believe in forcing the issue. After the hostilities broke out my father went to work for the War Production Board and we moved to Bethesda, just outside Washington, DC. I was sent to the Landon School, a very conventional institution. Upon entering the third grade, I had to learn to read fast, but I couldn't yet master the words *and* or *the*. Finally having accomplished that, the first complex words I learned after several trips to the bathroom were *American Standard*. I could read that even before tackling the likes of *Goodnight Moon*.

My climate-change-conscious daughter Elizabeth tells me she always follows the sensible suggestion left in a note on your bed each night asking you to inform the maid that you have no need for a fresh towel every day. However, Elizabeth points out, most hotels don't provide a hook for your wet towel. If you leave the towel draped over the tub it is sure to be whisked away and washed, Planet Earth unsaved.

I do like a bathroom with a window so that I can see palm trees swaying in the morning breeze or gaze at ocean waves as I brush my teeth. I don't play golf but that doesn't keep me from enjoying my favorite hotel guest room at the golf resort near Hangzhou, which has a bathroom that looks over the golf course, the tea plants, and the lake through a large window.

I have never understood the concept of freestanding reading lights placed near the center of night tables. Unless they are extremely bright, I find myself huddling in one corner of the bed, my book outstretched under a lampshade that's usually opaque. I prefer to read under an adjustable wall-mounted sconce that I can pull above my pillow. I don't understand why all hotels (and even the few friends I visit) don't have them. This doesn't mean I approve of those tiny wall-mounted bullet lights provided for reading after I've pushed a button and all the other lights in the room have automatically gone off, leaving no possibility of controlling one light manually to alleviate the gloom that results from one of those pin lights. I assume the bullet lights are there so you won't keep your partner awake as you finish another British cozy mystery. But after I've traveled eighteen hours on Cathay Pacific from New York to Hong Kong, forced to read under similar wretched contraptions, I am not about to endure the same experience in my bed.

When Bob Burns developed Four Seasons Hotel New York (which he sold in 1992), he created a separate dressing area with a great deal of hanging space, a large bureau, and plenty of room for you to set out your opened luggage. Sir Michael Kadoorie went a step further in his hotels, creating an even larger dressing room that had the marvelous feature of a closet that could be opened from the hall, where clothes that need to be cleaned or pressed could be picked up and returned without disturbing guests. No shoes in the hall waiting to be shined at any Peninsulas.

All this space for dressing is well and good but practically everyone I know travels nowadays with carry-on luggage—some, like me, with bags from Hartmann, and a select few with

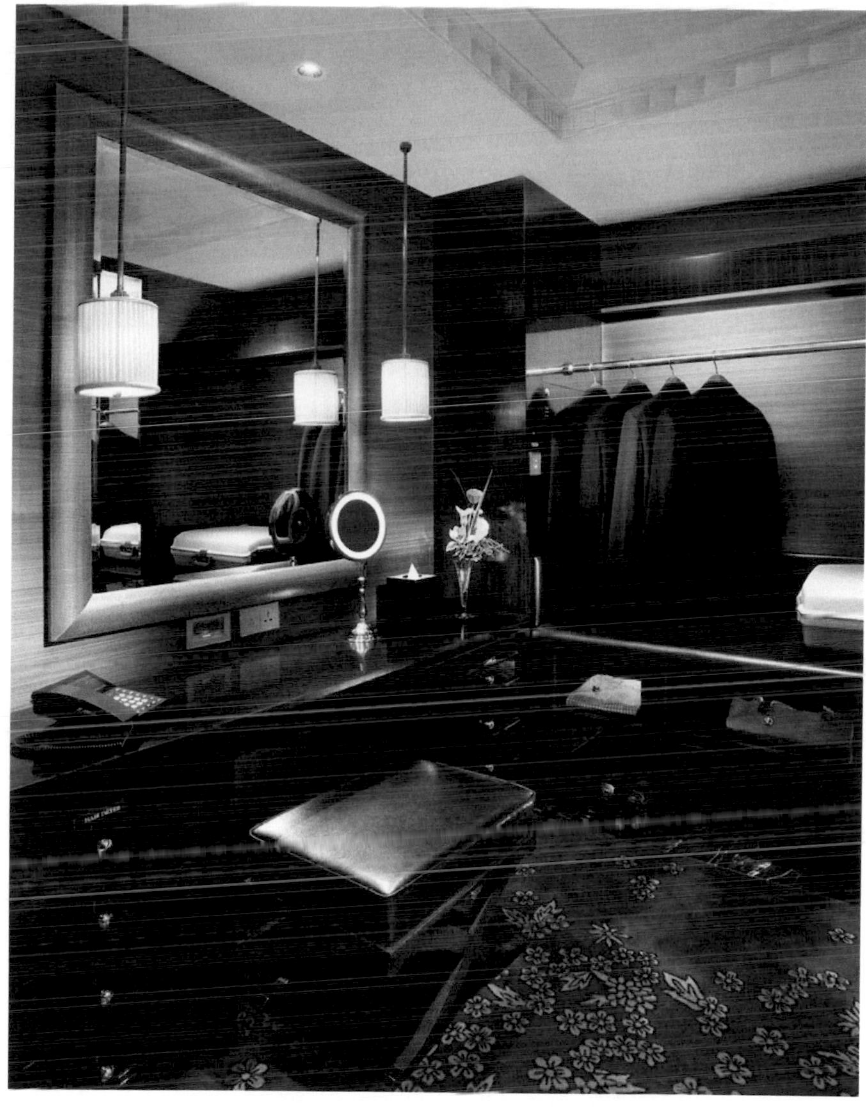

THE PENINSULA SHANGHAI.

The clothes in my carry-on suitcase get lost in this typical dressing area.

genuine Louis Vuitton, class on wheels. It seems to me that in most cases, the richer the person, the less they bring, unless they are going to a party or wedding, staying with friends for a week in a large country house in Scotland or perhaps a château in France. I often wonder what those people who wear shorts and flip-flops on airplanes carry in their enormous suitcases. A trip to Disneyland does not require a couple of ball gowns. In any event, these tourists are not hanging up their sweatshirts and jeans in Sir Michael's dressing rooms at Peninsulas. And it is doubtful that their quarters in Orlando will include a walk-in closet to accommodate their extensive wardrobes.

I have no need for so much space myself, but I once did have a memorable encounter with a walk-in closet, a very large walk-in closet. I was invited by President and Mrs. Eisenhower for a drink at their house in Palm Desert, asked not for myself goodness knows, but because I was staying with my in-laws who had a house nearby. They were intimate friends. Almost immediately Mrs. Eisenhower—Mamie, as she was known universally—invited me on a tour of her house. As is often the case on such tours in that fancy Southwest resort, the Eldorado Club, it included a view of the owners' dressing area. So I was not surprised when the former First Lady opened the door of her enormous walk-in closet and invited me to inspect her vast slacks collection. The closet contained nothing but dozens and dozens of neatly hung pants in every conceivable shade of pastel. After gazing at this I was literally speechless.

Few travelers will be blessed with either a dressing room or a walk-in closet. They will have to be content with the four-foot closet, which is the standard size for most chain hotels. This could present a problem for those couples traveling with three suitcases each. The closet's single shelf will be packed with blankets and extra pillows. On the floor of the closet rest a baggage rack, an ironing board, and a safe, the latter fine for others but not for me. I am terrified I would forget my combination or lose the key. Besides, the only valuable item I possess is an ancient non-working Rolex that's hidden somewhere in my bedroom, I no longer remember where. The estimate for having it fixed was four thousand dollars.

Finally in terms of regular closets, I am driven crazy by hangers that are attached to the pole and cannot be brought down conveniently for me to hang my pants and shirts. I don't like being thought of as a potential criminal every time I struggle to hang up my jacket from Zara. Another aspect of the design of guest room closets that's not fully thought out is the folding luggage rack, which is usually hidden far in the back. When I place my bag on top of this fragile contraption, the top part stands uneasily against the wall, hardly improving the paint job. More often, I open my bag on the bed bench. This isn't much better. The bench is never wide enough to accommodate my bag when it's open, so the top flops onto the bed. Since I have short legs, my foot movement is not impeded when I'm in bed, but the effect is hardly decorative.

Of course Peninsula guest rooms have technically advanced mechanisms. This is admirable, except for the technically challenged such as me. The lights, curtains, air-conditioning, television, even mood: All are directed by a control panel. No turning on a couple of lamps by hand, no flicking on your TV with a familiar home-like clicker. It's everything on or everything off. Impossible any other way. There are instructions placed low down somewhere beside the bed, but after a sixteen-hour flight from JFK, following them is beyond me. In the old days when I was checking into The Peninsula Hong Kong my first duty was to tell the bellboy what soap I would like. Hermès in my case. The second was to call the engineer to find out how to make the TV work. My daughter Elizabeth bemoans the lack of conveniently placed outlets to charge your devices in the room. Even I have been known to crawl along the floor removing an essential plug to charge my iPhone.

The grander the hotel, the fewer rooms with two beds. You will not find many of those in Peninsula hotels. But in a convention hotel, over 60 percent of rooms have two beds, partly because some companies want their employees to share a room, get to know each other better, and bond. When I was employed at Welton Becket & Associates I had to endure this a couple of times at a golf resort in Arizona ominously called The Wigwam. I bonded neither in the guest room nor on the golf course, where I was a fish way out of water. Holiday Inn developed the concept of the double-double room. This means two four-foot-six-inch-wide beds, allowing a family to share: parents in one bed, children in another. Not my idea of a great vacation. Nor is staying at any hotel called The Wigwam.

In Europe grand hotels such as The Gritti Palace in Venice have twin beds placed together so that topped with a king-sized mattress they can be used by a single person or a loving couple, and separated, by two friends who aren't romantically involved. Each time I stayed at the Gritti, I liked having the same room but I was able to be flexible with my choice of roommates and, occasionally, bedmate. Alone, I can survive quite nicely in a single bed. Every grand house I have ever visited has twin beds in its guest rooms. But what is acceptable at the Gritti and in a great house in Southampton or Palm Beach is not acceptable to most travelers these days.

The number of suites in a hotel is proportional to its grandness. In luxury hotels up to 30 percent of the accommodations may be in the form of suites, while convention hotels have very few. The typical two-room suite usually has a door connecting it to another room that has two beds for children. This is a definite upgrade from a family having to share one room with double doubles, Holiday Inn style. My favorite kind of suite is one where the bedroom opens up through an arch to the living area so that I can see and appreciate what I have paid for (or to be exact, upgraded to). I first stayed in this kind of suite at the Plaza Athénée in Paris, and when I redesigned the St. Regis I adapted it very successfully. I was upgraded to a suite at the former Ritz in Boston—now Taj Boston. Although the living room had a lovely view of the Common, the bedroom down the hall from it was small and rather mean. Since I spent most of my time in the bedroom with the TV on, I did not fully appreciate Taj's kindness.

The larger the suite, the fancier the name, all the way up to presidential and even imperial (for the emperor of Japan, presumably, now that Haile Selassie and the queen mother, last empress of India, have died). Executive and junior suites are often not much larger than a deluxe guest room. A regular suite occupies almost two full bays and should have a powder room so that guests don't see your discarded bath towels. As suites get larger, dining rooms, pantries, media rooms, gyms, and even swimming pools are added. When we were designing the presidential suite for the St. Regis, our aim was to provide the guest with the experience of living in a grand apartment on Fifth Avenue—where the hotel is situated, of course. The foyer, living room, dining room, library, and guest bedroom were created as if Brooke Astor herself resided there and had lent you the place for the weekend. In fact, by then she lived on Park Avenue, but I think the presidential suite's conventional elegance would have appealed to her.

As I noted, presidents visiting New York used to stay at the presidential suite at the Waldorf until a few years ago, when a Chinese insurance group bought the hotel. As for those royal suites, Near Eastern kings use them extensively, not only taking an adjacent room but occupying the entire floor. As for the European royals, a couple I know vaguely never pay for a room in a hotel, much less a grand suite. Most prefer to stay with friends who are all too happy to have them and the accompanying inconvenience in order to secure a footing on the ladder for what passes as social success in New York.

In any event, visiting royals, and Mrs. Astor for that matter, would find little familiar in the kind of presidential suites we are creating these days. The empress of Japan travels rarely; nevertheless the seven-bay suite my firm designed at the Mandarin Oriental, New York is called the empress suite. If she stayed there she would find herself in a world very different from that suite in the St. Regis. For a start, there are few square rooms. The foyer, living room, master bedroom, and guest bedrooms all have dramatically angled corner windows. A media room has been added in place of the formal paneled library. The master bath has two rain showers and floor-to-ceiling glass facing the populated park. In the end, although their styles are very different, the suites accomplish the same thing: They are both very grand indeed and make quite an impression.

My only experience of such luxury was the imperial suite at Le Grand Hotel in Rome. I was shown to its "swing" room. This is a room connected to all the grander suites so that an extra bedroom may be added if necessary or, if not, rented separately to another occupant. This "swing" room was on the second floor and had an extremely high ceiling, an appropriate chandelier, and a lavish décor similar to its imperial neighbor. I accepted it without hesitation. Before I went out to dinner that evening (alone since I was on a business trip), I discovered that the door between my "swing" room and the suite was unlocked. Since I was most certainly a repeat customer, I assumed that the error was made deliberately.

For dinner I went to Passato, a convivial restaurant near the Piazza Navona that no longer exists, and sat down at a table by myself. My neighbor was a nice-looking youngish man, and after we had chatted for a while he invited me to join him. His name was Edward and he'd been working with refugees in South Sudan. As our meal wound up, I thought an after-dinner drink in the imperial suite would make a nice change of pace. I robbed my horribly overpriced minibar (something that I almost never do), and very soon talk of the suffering in the Horn of Africa turned to lighter subjects. Under the high domed ceiling and glittering chandelier, surrounded as we were by damask-covered walls and silk curtains, our talk became lighter and lighter. Thus I enjoyed a relatively swinging evening in the grand living room at the imperial suite just off my swing room at Le Grand Hotel in Rome.

CHAPTER 7

ROOM SERVICE

Worth the Wait?

ONE OF MY EARLIEST AND INDEED fondest childhood memories is of being sick in bed and my mother bringing me meals on a blue tray—the kind with legs that allowed the plates and glass to remain stationary if I wiggled my feet. For some reason a vision of bread pudding milk toast flickers across my mind. I am sure that I was served three-minute soft-boiled eggs along with toast, made not from Wonder Bread but from Arnold white bread, enriched to be sure, but without the benefit of those lifesaving seven grains. Although we had a woman helping in the house, the meal was prepared and carried up by my mother. For me, it is a happy memory of a

ROOM SERVICE AT THE DORCHESTER IN LONDON.

mother's love for her child. It was the best room service I ever received.

Alas, it was practically the only room service I have ever enjoyed. I've never had breakfast in bed in a hotel. I visibly blanch at the prices asked. I will occasionally go downstairs for a bowl of blueberries and fat-free yogurt judiciously ordered from an à la carte menu, but I almost never spring for the huge buffets hotels provide for a stiff price. Usually I go around the corner and order a cup of coffee and a bun, the latter shared with Tyree. The only Starbucks I have ever graced is the one across the street from the Four Seasons in Shanghai, not an easy commute. Cars turn even when the light is against them, a fact that I never get used to, so I risk death for a reasonably priced cup of coffee, a shared bun, and a thirty-dollar savings. A penny earned . . .

In terms of hotel design I know exactly how room service works and works efficiently. Breakfast is prepared in the room service kitchen, which also provides food for the large all-day restaurant, formally and inaccurately known as the coffee shop. The restaurants in fancier hotels usually have their own kitchen, whether it's Italian, Chinese, or Continental. Accordingly the room service kitchen must be as near as possible to the service elevator so that food can be delivered as fast as possible. This is easy to achieve in a compact town hotel, but much less so in a resort, where the all-day restaurant and its kitchen have been placed far from the elevators in order to take advantage of the garden, the pool, and the view. Relative efficiency may be obtained, but the design planner must consider this necessity from the start. Many, many do not.

Most reviews of hotels in *The New York Times* report how

long it takes for breakfast once ordered to arrive in the room. I am generally consumed with tension about how many blocks my taxi can make between lights as I creep down Lexington from Ninetieth Street to Sixty-Second and Fifth to the Knickerbocker Club to meet a friend—or worse still, across Central Park to the Metropolitan Opera House—hoping for enough time for glass of wine before the curtain. I cannot see myself enduring the agitation of waiting for coffee and seven-grain toast, no butter please, to reach my room in less than twenty minutes. If I ever were to order breakfast, obeying those helpful notices that reside on my bed each night, I would most certainly have it served on a table, preferably at normal dining height in the living area, not in my bed. Since those golden days when my mother brought me my meals on a tray I have loathed both breakfast in bed and room service. Virtually none of my female friends agree. They rhapsodize about their breakfasts in bed at this or that hotel.

OLD

CHAPTER 8

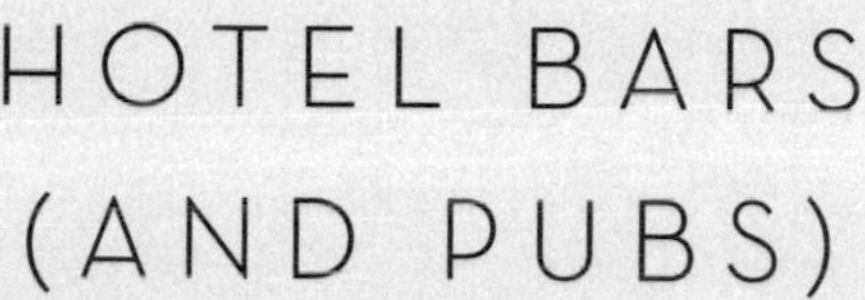

HOTEL BARS (AND PUBS)

WHETHER I'M RUSHING DOWN IN AN elevator or descending elegantly on a grand staircase, I'm often on my way to find a place to have a drink. I don't mean a martini or a cosmopolitan (I've never actually tried the latter, believe it or not); I mean a glass of white wine. In most hotels I am faced with the choice of having that Sancerre in either a lobby bar or what I call "a bar bar," a singular enclosed space that in the old days was most often wood-paneled, dark, and enclosed with doors that are opened a little before noon.

The Ritz London has a lobby bar of sorts made up of areas along the grand promenade that leads to The Ritz Restaurant, lined with couches and chairs grouped along the walls.

KING COLE BAR, THE ST. REGIS NEW YORK.

The original Ritz Bar in Paris circa 1950 (above) and the Four Seasons Blue Bar, Hong Kong, today (right).

Definitely not enclosed, but certainly elegant. In recent years a somewhat garish bar called The Rivoli was added, opening onto Piccadilly. It does not appeal to me at all, being somewhat out of character with César Ritz's masterful Louis XV design.

Virtually all Hiltons, Marriotts, and Sheratons have vast lobby bars, often with an atrium soaring above them. Again, at the Grand Hyatt Shanghai it's about sixty stories high, not making for a cozy place to sip a glass of Sancerre. As a rule these spaces remain fairly empty all day long, are hysterically busy at the cocktail hour, and are almost deserted at dinnertime.

Lobby bars are too open, too exposed, for me to sit there in complete comfort. I confess that sometimes I have a drink a bit before the yardarm has been crossed, particularly if I have arrived at a hotel before my room is ready. This is usually the case, and the Mr. Babbitt in me doesn't want the entire hotel to witness this early indulgence. But I think that after a sixteen-hour flight from JFK I am entitled. As I slip through the doors of an enclosed bar and settle down in a corner, I'm always greeted warmly by the bartender and heartily hailed as his first customer of the day, no value judgments included.

I absolutely love hotel bars. The first one I went to was the original Ritz Bar in Paris, the most famous in the world thanks to Ernest Hemingway and Scott and Zelda Fitzgerald. It used to

have its own entrance on the Rue Gambon, far from the main entrance to the hotel on the Place Vendôme. At lunchtime, sun streamed into the French-oak-paneled space while bartenders in spotless white jackets attended to incredibly well-dressed chattering customers. I couldn't have been exactly penniless as a youth since I spent a surprising amount of time in this bar, drinking martinis (I did back then), enjoying the truly glamorous surroundings, and looking at the fashionable people.

In the summer of 1953 I stopped in with my school and college friend Godfrey Truslow before we went to Joan Dillon-Moseley's wedding. We were so intoxicated by the surroundings, and probably our martinis, too, that we lost track of time. We were very late getting to the Madeleine—so late, in fact, that as we climbed up the church's broad steps, the immense bronze doors opened and we were almost knocked down by the happy (or so we thought) bride and groom. Unfortunately the marriage did not last, nor did the Ritz Bar. It was destroyed in order to make way for the hotel's casino entrance. Now the hotel has the tiny Bar Hemingway on the Rue Gambon side and a much larger, lounge-like bar at the hotel entrance. Even though the entire hotel has been stunningly redesigned by Thierry Despont and is the talk of Paris and beyond, nothing can replace what was once the most famous, historic, and glamorous bar in the world: the Ritz Bar.

Despite my enthusiasm for the old Ritz Bar, I was never a regular, so I didn't become friends with the two bartenders. Nor would I have warranted their attention, being that I was a small student in a seersucker jacket and chino pants (probably gray flannel for the Ritz). In those days people noticed such distinctions.

Besides the concierge, the person at a hotel who is most likely to become your new best friend, the person who will remember your name after a ten-year absence, is the bartender. In 2011 I visited the tiny, cozy corner bar, one of my favorites, in De L'Europe Amsterdam on the Amstel Canal. It had been renovated and opened up since my last visit, and was decidedly less cozy. But the bartender Dirk, whom I have known for twenty-five years, remained as affable and charming as ever, exuding the warmth that was possessed by that once perfect cozy hotel bar. In New York the popular art deco Bemelmans Bar at the Carlyle is decorated with delightful murals of Central Park by Ludwig Bemelmans, creator of the classic Madeline children's books. They fail, however, to negate my feeling of claustrophobia caused by the oppressively low ceiling that looms over the bar's rather large space. My feeling is shared, it seems, by few others, as the place is almost always packed at night.

After thirty years no one knows me anymore at the St. Regis, except the bartender at the King Cole Bar. While the old Ritz Bar may have been the most famous in the world, the King Cole Bar may be the best known in New York, if not the country. When I was asked to redesign the hotel, it was no longer where it is now, in full view of the check-in lobby. That bar had been replaced by a bookstore devoted almost exclusively to the subject of automobiles, a topic that did not engage me since I no longer drove cars. Out went the store and others, and the King Cole Bar was restored with its Maxfield Parrish mural hanging in its former position over the bar. The bar is my contribution to the serious and not too serious drinkers of the world, and it is extremely popular. Its fame rests largely on Parrish's enormous painting, vividly depicting the jolly king surrounded by his courtiers. This is not a serious subject that might unsettle the nightly crowd of drinkers.

The only hotel bar I can think of that is more popular than the King Cole Bar is the Captain's Bar at the Mandarin Oriental, Hong Kong. The Chinese are not really bar-goers, and those that

HOTEL METROPOLE, BRUSSELS.
A good place to celebrate New Year's Eve.

I created in Peninsulas in China, Bangkok, and Hong Kong are only moderately successful. It's not the local Chinese who are drawn to this windowless corner space of the Mandarin Oriental in central Hong Kong. The crowd is almost entirely expat British, a people not known for their abstinence. In Hong Kong they like to do their drinking in a very tony hotel.

Although I prefer to do my drinking in enclosed hotel bars, developers for some reason often do not include them in their plans, partly because they require an additional bartender, often my new and oldest best friend. Virtually all hotels have large lobby bars, usually in full sight of the front desk and often the elevators. I am not that averse to public imbibing in an open space, as I have said. My first experience of this took place at The Peninsula Hong Kong. It is a grand space divided by the hotel entrance. My only problem is that I have never found out which is the chic side to sit on. I'm afraid I must confess a major character flaw in that I care about where I am seated, especially in certain restaurants like the sorely missed Swifty's (in the back room) and La Grenouille (in the front room). At The Ritz Restaurant in London I can only hope to be seated next to the window, for I would never be so crass as to ask the maître d' Luigi for such an honor, despite my sixty years of loyalty to the place. Fortunately he honors that loyalty.

I am a traditionalist when it comes to the design and layout of a hotel bar. I like my bars straight, preferably with at least one corner where I can sit in case I happen to find someone to converse with. Barstools should have backs for comfort. I dislike circular bars where you have to avoid eye contact with the people seated across from you. The Palm Court in The Plaza, in a vain attempt to make that world-famous grand space more popular and relevant, has installed such a bar, one more suitable for the Holiday Inn in Sandusky, Ohio.

Grand hotels used to serve pitted green olives and delicious crisp, salty potato chips accompanied by dainty linen napkins (The Gritti Palace in Venice still does). But now most places seem to serve a variety of trail mix; you will find it not only in Sandusky but also on the Avenue Montaigne.

Occasionally I extend my hotel drinking beyond the cozy bar or lofty lobby lounge. I used to sip my Sancerre in what I call a grand café bar, such as the sleek, I. M. Pei–designed space of the Four Seasons in New York. Far less restrained and considerably more boisterous, two of my favorites are in the Alvear Palace Hotel in Buenos Aires and Hotel Metropole in Brussels. In BA the entire city seems to find its way into this high-ceilinged space off the lobby (at least those inhabitants who can afford to live in that area near the Jockey Club and French embassy, moving to their villas in Punta del Este in nearby Uruguay during the season). The Brussels Metropole bar is delightfully overdone and has served as a solution to the challenge of New Year's Eve two years running. No terrorist will keep me from enjoying one of my favorite festive hotel bars in the near or distant future.

Last winter I took my grandchildren Nuala and Orla to The Polo Lounge at The Beverly Hills Hotel in Los Angeles. I wanted them to see one of the few places left where you can savor the spirit of Old Hollywood. I told them about the times I had spent lounging around the hotel's busy-busy pool and about the days their mother and the family had spent in Bungalow 10. I felt confident that at least The Polo Lounge had survived intact despite the hotel's many renovations since those days. We were unceremoniously banished to an outer room crammed with tourists where there was not a single vestige of its famous green banana leaf wallpaper to be seen. Interestingly, when the hotel opened in 1924, the movie colony was not allowed into The Polo Lounge or even permitted to own property in the newly incorporated city. Only after Douglas Fairbanks managed by some mistake to buy an apartment there was the restriction lifted. Louis B. Mayer and Jack Warner were among the first to build mansions for themselves, and soon many stars followed their lead. The Polo Lounge became their refuge from gawking tourists. We were tourists, but there was nothing for us to gawk at, not even a green banana leaf.

I have given advice about finding affordable hotels that share their location with grand hotels like the Ritz in Paris. In Vienna, when Tyree and I stayed in Le Méridien across the Ringstrasse from the Opera House and the city's famous Hotel Sacher (yes, of Sacher torte fame), we shared not only the best location with that hotel but also its Blaue Bar, which is very small, pleasantly cluttered, and extremely cozy, a classic bar bar and one of the best in the town. Although we went there every evening before going out to dinner, the bartender realized we weren't staying at the hotel since we paid by credit card, not by giving him our room number. Still, he treated us as one of his own, every night reserving for us the same table and chilling the same Austrian Riesling. I suppose I could call this not bar-hopping but bar-borrowing.

Less traditionally designed and in fact rather gaudy is one of my favorite grand café bars, the Blue Bar at the Four Seasons Hotel Hong Kong. The funky décor aside, the views across the bay are extremely impressive, increasingly so as more skyscrapers are added to the skyline. They now dwarf the Peninsula, which used to be the Kowloon landmark in the 1970s. The crowd is as lively as you could wish, perhaps even a bit more so. But all

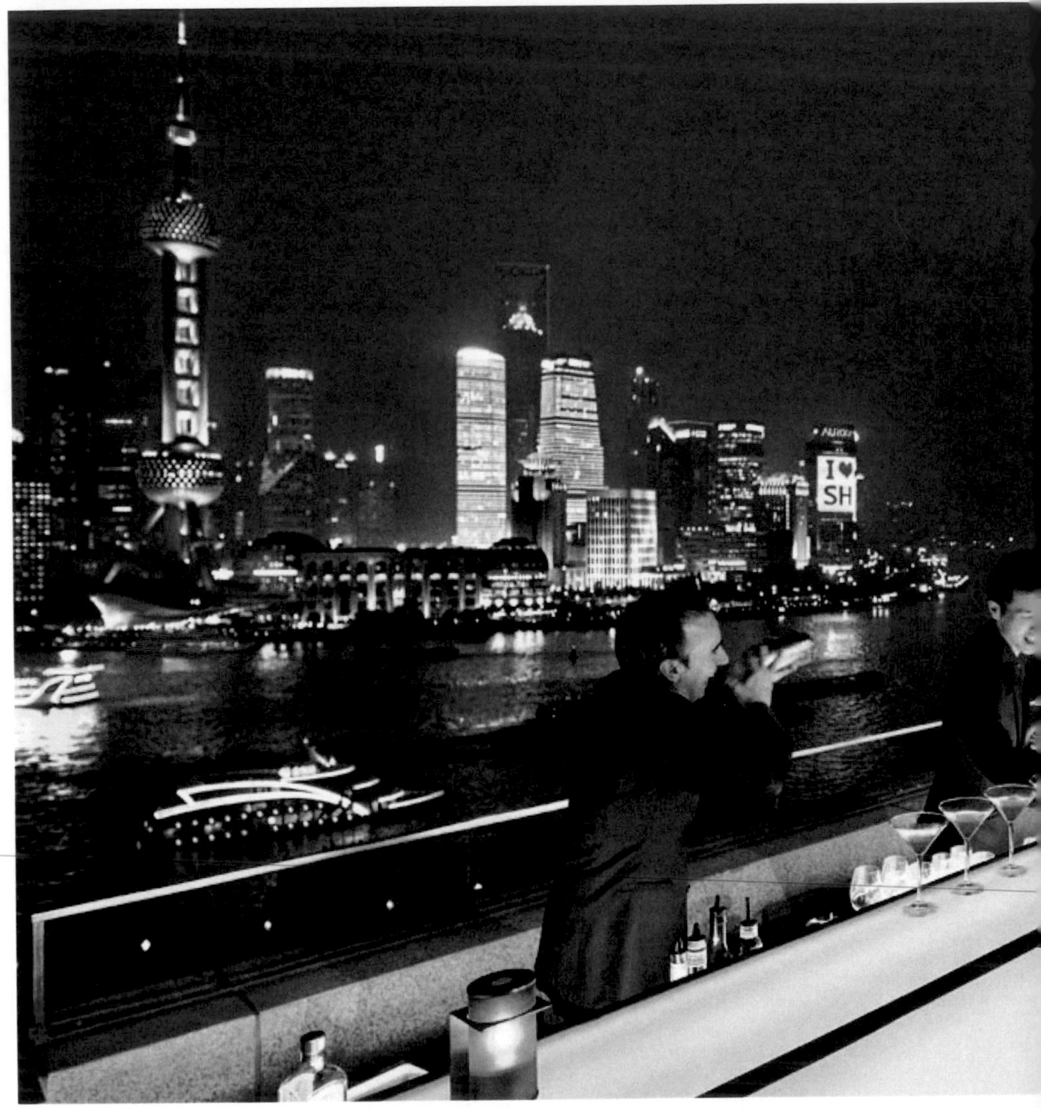

are very amicable. The first time I checked into this Four Seasons I made my first friend there. As usual I was down in the bar waiting for my room to be ready when Agnes, my server (formerly known as my waitress), asked my name before pouring me a glass of Sancerre. After this brief encounter, I returned to the lobby to collect the key to discover that the entire staff there already knew

Rooftop bar at The Peninsula Shanghai.

my name. In an instant the Blue Bar and the Four Seasons became one of my favorite bars and hotels in the world. "Nice to see you, Mr. Beer." With that, I was sold on the hotel. I am easy.

Recently I watched an episode of the British mystery series

Midsomer Murders on television. One scene takes place in a particularly fetching drinking establishment located in a village inn. I was reminded that one of my favorite places to imbibe is in a low-ceilinged, fire-crackling British pub. If, like me, you are an avid fan of that particular British mystery series or others such as *Inspector Lewis*, *Father Brown*, and *Grantchester*, you know that in most installments there will be a shot of a charming village pub with a picturesque thatched roof and a floor of rooms above the bar. I must confess, appealing as those village pubs are, I've never actually stayed in one, so I am not an expert on the amenities, but I'm certain the rooms do not rival those of the Ritz in London or Madrid. However, I do think it would be fine to chow down on a ploughman's lunch, the crusty sandwich that comes filled with Stilton (not cheddar for me), or a steak and kidney pie, accompanied by a pint of bitter, properly served at room temperature and without a head of bubbles, before retiring to a cozy room upstairs.

I MAY NEVER HAVE stayed at a village pub inn, but I did spend time at The Royal Castle Hotel on the quay in charming (again) Dartmouth in glorious South Devon. The hotel has a pub, with an appropriately low wood-beamed ceiling, where pints of bitter and ploughman's are dispensed to a crowd of enthusiastic locals. The guest rooms are reasonably sized but I would have preferred it if the hotel had had an elevator, because on my first stay I was placed on the fourth floor. On my next visit I made sure to take a room on the second floor, which, oddly, had its window open onto the corridor and the much-used stairs. The room was light-years better than the windowless one I was once given in Baghdad, and I do not remember being disturbed by the jocular crowd in the pub directly below. The countryside in South Devon is ravishing: green hills and hedges bordering the sparkling sea. And there is always that slow boat that takes you up the scenic, serene Dart River to Agatha Christie's country hilltop house, Greenway, an essential trip for fans of the queen of mysteries. Far below, by the river, is the boathouse where the murder is committed in *Dead Man's Folly.* The view of the river bend from the terrace is a treat even if you are not an Agatha Christie addict.

THE CHERUB INN, DARTMOUTH, UK

It's as cute as the name.

CHAPTER 9

HOTEL DINING

Often a Main Attraction

IN EVELYN WAUGH'S NOVEL *BRIDESHEAD Revisited,* when Charles Ryder asks Cordelia Marchmain, the sister of his great love Julia, out for dinner in London, he takes her to The Ritz Restaurant. In those days it was virtually the only socially acceptable place for members of a certain class to dine outside their own homes. In modern times we know Princess Margaret often occupied the south corner table on the park. Princess Diana liked the corresponding table on the north, where she usually had lunch with her great lady friend from Brazil. On my sixtieth birthday, as a treat, I was placed with Tyree at the table next to her. Unfortunately I never really had much of a look at the princess. I had, for once, faced my guest toward the corner so that

THE RITZ RESTAURANT, LONDON.

the birthday boy could enjoy a view of that glorious, garland-festooned room. In such company I was required to be a gentleman so I never turned and stared at what I was told was a vision in powder blue with matching blue shoes and handbag.

During the 1950s and 1960s there were many celebrated hotel restaurants in the United Kingdom and Europe, but most Americans felt that in their own country the last place they'd choose to eat was a hotel dining room. There were some exceptions, of course. During my years at Harvard, life for a select few revolved around the restaurant at the Ritz, which was regally located overlooking the Boston Common on one side and the fancy shops of Newbury Street on the other. I don't think the Cabots, the Lowells, and the Winthrops knew that there was any other place to dine outside their houses as they habitually sipped from those blue water glasses in that second-floor room. The Ritz is now the Taj, and that restaurant is now reserved for parties, and the Cabots and all have moved on, probably no farther than the nearby Somerset Club, which is also on the Common.

Boston was not alone in having just one cherished hotel restaurant. Tucked inside the Washington Ritz-Carlton, a hotel we renovated in 1995 (now The Fairfax at Embassy Row), was the Jockey Club where twenty-five years ago you might have found Kay Graham and Buffy Cafritz planning fundraisers. In Chicago, despite its wonderful restaurants, the old guard, including near neighbor the indomitable Mrs. Walter (Pussy) Paepcke, favored The Cape Cod Room in The Drake. In San Francisco the place to be seen was, surprisingly, Trader Vic's. Every morning you could read in the *Chronicle* about Mrs. Charles Fay—Frances—and with whom she had spent the previous evening, always, of course, at Trader Vic's.

During the 1960s and 1970s the hotels I was designing for Hilton, Sheraton, and Marriott had restaurants that failed to attract such lofty visitors. In fact they attracted almost no one at all. Those hotels had an all-day dining area that was large enough to accommodate most of the guests for breakfast, but too cavernous to appeal to them for lunch, and certainly not for dinner. Most of these hotels had an additional specialty restaurant, often serving Italian food and decked out with wood paneling, chandeliers, huge heavy unmovable chairs, and thick linen tablecloths. In other words: fancy and forgettable and undesirable unless you happened to be in downtown Atlanta on a rainy Sunday night. Dining alone in an almost deserted restaurant at the Ritz-Carlton seemed to me a more comforting choice than being adventurous and venturing forth to Miss Pittypat's Porch, always packed with tourists.

Somehow my parents, Fay and Wally Beer, never received the word that no one dined in hotel restaurants. In the distant days when Saturday lunch was an institution and the kind of people who now say they never drink at lunch drank plenty, usually martinis, my parents spent many a winter afternoon tucked into a cozy banquette in the window of The Sherry-Netherland's bar. At least one gin martini (no wine in those days) would be followed by eggs Benedict with ham, not smoked salmon. These days the martini would be replaced by a Bellini, the eggs by risotto primavera, followed by a bill from Arrigo Cipriani that would have discouraged my parents from dining in a hotel restaurant ever, ever again.

While Americans were reluctant to dine in hotels, in Europe there was no such prejudice against it. In Chartres and Dijon, the Michelin-starred restaurants were in two Best Western hotels, Le Grand Monarque and the Chapeau Rouge. They both served delicious food, although I wish the cooking had been regional rather than consisting of mystery concoctions dreamed up in the attempt to gain an additional star. Where was my *boeuf bourguignon* in Burgundy?

I would not expect to find *boeuf bourguignon* on the menu at the grand palace hotels in Paris. Formerly they had dazzling, opulent restaurants, such as L'Espadon at the Ritz, La Regence at the Plaza Athénée, and Les Ambassadeurs at Hôtel de Crillon, among others, which in my expense account days I often enjoyed. When I was designing a hotel in the Soviet Union I would take the last Air France plane from Moscow to Paris and rush to the Plaza Athénée, getting there just before the kitchen closed at the discreetly elegant La Regence. I'd often find it empty, except occasionally I'd see a large group of black-garbed veiled ladies huddled around a table under the huge central chandelier, silently sipping fruit juice.

Times have changed for those grand Paris restaurants. Star chefs have been employed—in the case of the Plaza Athénée, Alain Ducasse. The old dining room's single chandelier has been replaced by six decorated with long filaments that appear to be hanging in midair. The room is all white. The Dover sole on the menu has been replaced by M. Ducasse's creations, which shall remain mysterious to me, as I never will rustle up the nerve or the euros to enjoy them. But the restaurants, even without me, are fully booked.

In the United States we now have our share of opulent hotel restaurants, although few of them are in grand palace hotels. One notable exception was Lespinasse at the St. Regis when the hotel reopened in 1994. Although it's not the case in Europe, American hotel companies insist that their restaurants have a street entrance. The idea is to make customers think they are in a regular restaurant and forget their long-standing prejudice against dining at a hotel. In the case of the St. Regis this was not possible because we had created Astor Court, the two-story lobby that replaced the one on Fifth Avenue. The solution was to hire a fabulous chef, Gray Kunz, who received a four-star rating from *The New York Times*, encouraging people to come inside and dine splendidly. And they did for a while, until the recession. Then the cost of the special three-million-dollar kitchen, complete with sleek Molteni stoves that had been installed just for Mr. Kunz, could no longer be sustained. Like the restaurant at the Ritz-Carlton in Boston, the space that housed Lespinasse is now a party room, a victim of the downturn and most people's desire for less formal dining. Added to the difficulty is the fact that unlike most restaurants, hotels have to pay their staff union wages in addition to other expenses.

Today most hotel restaurants are a great deal plainer than they used to be. Gone are the crystal chandeliers, the lush curtains, the soft carpets, and even the tablecloths. The look is now clean, uncluttered, and in many cases very handsome, even dramatic. Unfortunately, with so many hard surfaces, the sound level is appalling. Several years ago I was dining with my family at Mercer Kitchen, the basement restaurant in The Mercer in Soho. The noise was deafening, and I soon gave up trying to communicate with my grandchildren; instead I amused myself watching two young women at the next table, each with cellphone in hand and talking away, probably to each other. It was perhaps the only way they could communicate. A long way from the Plaza Athénée and those veiled ladies in black at La Regence.

In terms of hotel restaurants, I'm a traditionalist in some ways. I'm still thrilled by the sight of a gleaming white tablecloth in any restaurant, be it simple or grand, that still bothers to cover its tables. Most stylish, madly popular restaurants ask you to eat their mystery meals on wood, stone, or, worse still, metal. Not that I'm nostalgic for the days when Hilton, Sheraton, and Marriott had upscale "specialty" restaurants traditionally decorated, of course, with huge tables covered with two layers of tablecloths and set with enormous padded high-backed chairs, making it almost impossible to move without calling a waiter. Even though those overly large tables were widely spaced, it was hard to hear your guests across them. When Lespinasse opened, even before the places were set I would run around turning the tables for two so that diners could face each other across the short side, closer together and within talking distance. I could do nothing about the vast round tables in the middle of the room, or the unmovable chairs. My attempt to make that grand restaurant more comfortable was not appreciated by the staff of Sheraton. But at least I knew its chairman Rand Araskog might understand my preference for small tables. He often ate at La Grenouille, where he looked perfectly happy dining on their appropriately small ones and sitting on one of their simple wood-backed chairs.

Another restaurant with reasonably sized tables is Majorelle, definitely inside a hotel, The Lowell on East Sixty-Third Street.

This laudable virtue is not surprising as its director is Charles Masson who, before his falling-out with his mother and brother, was the creative force behind La Grenouille. Charles and his designers have created a beautiful, classically designed restaurant. The Masson brothers may not be speaking but the two manage to continue the tradition of fine French dining started by their father at Le Pavillon, the 1939 World's Fair restaurant.

Since I often eat by myself, there is no need for me to try to communicate with someone over a meal. One of the special attractions of a hotel restaurant is that it is a good place to dine alone. Man or woman should never feel conspicuous since there are always single travelers scattered about the room. For me dining by myself is a positive pleasure: no forced conversation, no interruptions from my enjoyment of the food. I find it a good time to contemplate my future, which always seems brighter after a glass or two of wine. I am rather famous for daring to eat at La Grenouille by myself, well seated up front in "the frog pond," dreaming without distraction or worry about paying for someone else's meal in that not inexpensive, flower-filled, deliciously Old World restaurant.

Far from the realm of red banquettes and exquisite flowers was the dining room at the Hotel Leningrad where, on a business trip during the Soviet era, I found myself eating alone. The reaction was curious. The staff, a group of idle men smoking in the corner, was apparently completely unused to seeing a man dining without the company of business associates or drinking buddies. The waiters assumed that I must be there to solicit a woman, helpfully to be supplied before I respectfully declined. No such propositions would ever have been made at La Grenouille.

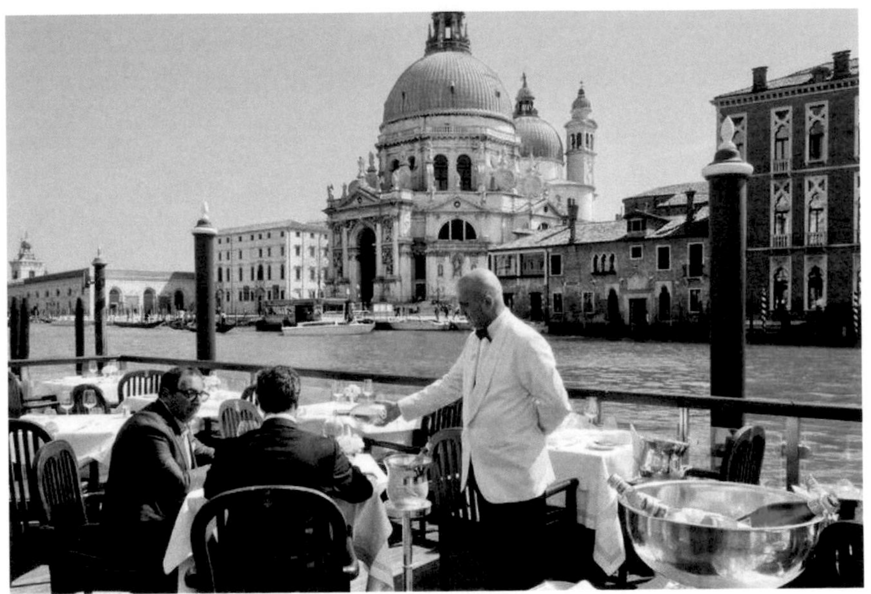

THE GRITTI PALACE HOTEL IN VENICE.

As a matter of fact, when I wrote that I would never be propositioned at La Grenouille, I wasn't entirely accurate. More than a few of its customers take where they are seated in the restaurant very seriously. For those who care, the tables up front on the right side when you enter are the most prized. The first table for four is the best and might accommodate Mercedes Bass or Leonard and Judy Lauder, while at the first table for two next to it in the corner, Henry Kissinger can be found, but never the likes of me. One afternoon I came in rather late and was shown to that very table, an offer I eagerly accepted. Amazed that this bespectacled, bald, elderly man was so honored, the couple next to me asked, "Who are you? You must be somebody." Soon a very attractive young woman came up and said that she and her friend would like to meet me later and wanted my phone number. It just proves that you can be somebody as long as you are well seated: *bien placé.*

La Grenouille is not part of a hotel although four years ago I did a plan to incorporate the restaurant into the adjacent office building, which was to be converted into a hotel. That never happened, but perhaps just the idea justifies my including it in this hotel chronicle. Perfect as the restaurant is, it would be even more perfect if it had a terrace for dining outdoors when the weather is wonderful. My mind is filled with memories of happy lunches on terraces of hotels such The Gritti Palace on the Grand Canal, the De L'Europe in Amsterdam on a somewhat less grand canal, Le Sirenuse in Positano looking over the town and the Mediterranean, and the vastly simpler Apollon Suites Hotel in Karystos on the edge of the Aegean Sea.

In 1960, having traveled to Taormina third class on a train standing much of the way, I discovered that my simple *pensione* was almost next to the town's one grand hotel, in those distant days the San Domenico, which had a marvelous terrace looking over the ancient Roman amphitheater and the Ionian Sea below. In the immediate foreground, in fact at the very next table to mine, sat Ingrid Bergman with her lovely and, for me, appropriately aged daughter Pia Lindstrom. Even though I had traveled third class, I looked reasonably appropriate, too: clean tan chino pants, blue Brooks Brothers button-down shirt, and a striped seersucker jacket. Three nights running I sat alone, smiling shyly and ever hopeful that an invitation to join them would be extended. Of course Miss Bergman had left her doctor husband in Sweden for the Italian film director Roberto Rossellini and was not interested in anyone else or anything appropriate. I had to be content with enjoying the view from that sublime hotel terrace. Not a tragedy, but still . . .

Nor is dining on the terrace of the Hotel Ritz, Madrid a tragedy, to say the very least. After last year's trip I have decided that eating there on a terrace elevated above the enclosed garden is one of my favorite hotel dining experiences. If I had been seated in the garden below, I would have been served tapas. I have to confess that I may be the only person in the world who is not devoted to those little plates, so I opted for white tablecloths and a less local menu under the shade of enormous trees and the Ritz-blue awnings. Gracious living on a budget, sort of, since the menu encouraged half portions, more than enough for me.

Staying at the Ritz recalled the style to which I had become accustomed in days gone by. On more recent trips I have stayed in simpler hotels, especially in Europe. In the 1960s when I visited Paris, Rome, or Athens I stayed in small hotels that didn't have restaurants, among them the Lenox and the Université on the Left Bank. Today, in the United

HOTEL RITZ, MADRID.

Sitting above the garden is one of my favorite places for lunch.

States I wouldn't stay in establishments like those offered by Choice Hotels or Hampton Inn, since they are not "full service" and only offer breakfast. All very comfortable, I'm sure, but unless I can have a simple meal they would not afford me the pleasure I get when I'm staying in a hotel where I can have a slice of pizza and a glass of red wine before retiring to bed. A Sleep Inn is not and never will be my lodging of choice.

In the Far East travelers take many of their meals in hotels. Even the simplest Chinese ones not branded Sheraton, Hilton, or

CAPRICE, FOUR SEASONS HONG KONG.

The view from my table, number 44.

Marriott have several places to eat, usually a steak house, an Italian, and a vast Chinese, along with as many as forty private dining rooms and, of course, the all-day, all-night restaurant.

Often the world's most celebrated interior designers have had a hand in creating stylish contemporary spaces for the most upscale hotels. In New York, Tony Chi designed the lovely restaurant Asiate, which added luster to my planning of the Mandarin Oriental. Although its designer is unknown to me, no hotel restaurant is more dazzling than my favorite, Caprice, a glittering, glamorous confection—far from minimally designed—on the sixth floor of the Four Seasons Hotel Hong Kong. Some diners may enjoy staring at the view of the harbor and the new skyscrapers beyond. I prefer sitting away from the windows on the red velvet banquette at table 44, enjoying the sight of the glass floor and the sparkling chandeliers. Far from the languid feeling evoked when you dine at the serenely tasteful Ritz Restaurant in London, Caprice, an over-the-top bauble in the least traditional and most jazzy city in the world, produces an experience that is nothing short of exhilarating. Sitting on the banquette, remembering the time when almost everyone except my parents said that they would never deign to eat in a hotel restaurant, as I'm waited upon by a solicitous staff and surrounded by elegantly dressed locals, I enjoy hotel dining at its most sumptuous and delicious best.

CHAPTER 10

BALLROOMS AND MEETING ROOMS

HOTEL BALLROOMS ARE COLUMN FREE spaces where you can go to dance for fun, such as at the Waltz Evenings at Boston's Copley Plaza I attended as a Harvard undergraduate, or for a more serious cause, like raising money for Evelyn Lauder's Breast Cancer Research Foundation at the Waldorf Astoria. Even if the ballrooms are vast, as much as fifty thousand square feet and more, they remain column-free. Because hotels like the Ritz in London and Paris are built on constricted lots, they haven't had the large open space needed for a ballroom. But in 2007 The Ritz London, after taking over a stately eighteenth-century house next door, acquired a modest ballroom there. The newly renovated Ritz

BALLROOM OF THE ST. REGIS GRAND IN ROME.

Paris, which reopened its doors in 2016, now has an underground ballroom that can accommodate four hundred guests. Meanwhile, the Carlyle in New York doesn't have a genuine ballroom; it's more like a fancy meeting room. No vaulted domes or hanging chandeliers in that low-ceilinged space.

A few of Europe's grand palace hotels do have sumptuous ballrooms. One of the most impressive is in The St. Regis Rome, despite its odd location across from the Termini Train Station far from the tourist centers around the Via Veneto and the Spanish Steps. Nevertheless because of the grandeur of its ballroom, during the winter The St. Regis Rome becomes the political and social center of Rome with everyone gathering under its vaults and chandeliers. The Continental in Paris has an equally grand ballroom, although to locate it these days you would have to find it under the hotel's new name, The Westin Paris-Vendôme, on the corner of the Rue de Rivoli facing the Tuileries. I would have preferred it if Starwood had not slapped *Westin* in front of the *Europa* in Venice and Rome's Excelsior. In *La Dolce Vita*, Marcello Mastroianni and friends tootled down the Via Veneto in their flashy convertibles in front of the Excelsior, no chain hotel name needed. And although I am somewhat responsible for the creation of the St. Regis brand, as our renovation was so successful, I am glad to say that the St. Regis Hotel in New York proudly retains its original name, as opposed to Le Grand Hotel in Rome. That hotel first changed its name to the St. Regis Grand and recently to The St. Regis Rome. Gone are all vestiges of that original name, which symbolized elegance and tradition since 1893. Somehow the name is less grand. Westin Excelsior indeed.

Virtually all ballrooms these days are designed to be easily divided up so that the whole large column-free space can accommodate many hundreds of people at the same time; with the help of sliding partitions, smaller rooms suitable for parties of fifty or fewer can be created. Flexible, yes, although gone are the vaults, recessed ceiling panels, and low-hanging chandeliers. The challenge for the designer is to create rooms that have style and glamour, even if the walls have to be moved.

I was once honored in the Empire Room of the Waldorf by the Preservation League of New York for my work preserving a number of historic hotels in the city. As per my instructions, there were no projected images and none of the laudatory speeches that plague such evenings, thank you. The first time I ever honored anyone was at the St. Regis Roof. I was eighteen and I felt geeky in my white tie and tails as I escorted Susannah Ryan there to her coming-out party. To be sure, I was her second escort. My role was to toast her parents, Mr. and Mrs. Peter Fortune Ryan. That was the occasion when I discovered Valium. Last year I swallowed a couple before a talk in front of a Hospitality Design convention in Las Vegas that was held in a large meeting room inside an enormous divisible ballroom at the Mandalay Bay. It was quite a different occasion and far from the sedate evening I spent with the Ryans, Lester Lanin playing "Just One of Those Things" on the St. Regis Roof more than sixty years before.

About thirty years ago the St. Regis Roof was threatened when the management group at Sheraton in Boston, not too sympathetic toward the world of Lester Lanin's society band so beloved by the Upper East Side crowd, decided to trash the Roof and turn it into luxury suites. I objected strenuously to no avail. It was saved, but only because one day my eye doctor John Espy and his wife Polly invited me to dinner at the very last minute after a guest had canceled. Happy to attend, I was seated next to a woman I hadn't met before and whose name, as usual, I did not catch. She dutifully asked me what I was working on and I told her about the St. Regis and that I was upset because the Roof was to be destroyed. At that point the unknown woman left the table, made a phone call to the president of Sheraton, and the Roof was saved. My dinner partner turned out to be Jessie Araskog, the wife of the chairman of ITT Sheraton, Rand Araskog.

Whether you are attending a party, business function, or charity event in a ballroom, there is always an area immediately adjacent that serves drinks and a bit of food before the doors open to the main event. This space is somewhat inelegantly known as the pre-function area. It is ideally about one-third the size of the ballroom, with easy access to the kitchen for drinks and hors d'oeuvres service. Although there's a major effort these days to design ballrooms that have windows giving onto the outdoors, most are still internal. The cocktail area usually has a great many windows and ideally even an outdoor terrace where you can mingle with friends or, if you're alone, stroll around smiling and trying at least to look popular.

Ballroom complexes invariably contain meeting rooms for business or entertaining. Often they are rather plain with all sorts of technical equipment for projecting graphs and making conference calls. I have not mastered the art of working this on my own, regrettably. It was not long ago for me that even making a cellphone call was a challenge until the iPhone entered my new twenty-first-century life. Of course not all meeting rooms are utilitarian and business-like. Five years ago I saw some at the

Four Seasons Beijing that were very contemporary but at the same time glamorous, with fabulous light fixtures and rich combinations of wood, stone, and fabric. Business does not have to be undertaken in dull surroundings.

I have planned many meeting rooms but my most memorable is one at the St. Regis. Although many designers these days are minimalists, a few subscribe to the theory that you can never do too much. In historic terms, whoever designed the interior of the Travellers Club on the Champs-Élysées in Paris, which includes a malachite staircase, certainly subscribed to that theory. The Fontainebleau Room at the St. Regis does not go that far, and its carved cornices and pilasters, its abundance of gilt, multiple mirrors, and shimmering chandeliers may or may not be too much, but they certainly add up to a lot, thanks to my genius partner Gustin Tan at BBGM. I have given several parties, including one for my daughter Elizabeth's engagement, in that room, which is placed so far at the end of all the other meeting rooms that I wonder if anyone ever sees it. Too bad, since it is quite special.

I have spent many nights of my life escorting women to charity events, but am seldom taken by them. I would never make it as a true "walker," to my financial disadvantage. I have always paid my way. I know that most often after a woman has checked her coat, she will disappear into the ladies' room to repair her looks, even if she's been in a taxi for less than ten minutes. When I run into the men's room, it is not to comb my nonexistent hair but for a reason related to my age. Among the many practical considerations to be addressed when designing a ballroom complex is the placement of the bathroom. In my designs I have never put the door in full view of the cocktail area, since I'm not interested in the assembled drinkers making note of that particular maneuver. A minor nicety perhaps, but a nicety nevertheless.

This brings me to the question of hotel public toilets. It might seem somewhat indelicate of me to provide a discussion of them here, but as my years on earth zoom past eighty-three I've developed a growing interest in such facilities. One of my pet peeves about dining out in New York and most cities in fact is the need to go down a flight of stairs, sometimes one that spirals, to get to the bathrooms. At the St. Regis, those that service the lobby bar and restaurants are below. When we renovated the hotel, there was not enough space to accommodate more than a small coat closet on the main floor, much less a bathroom, but at least we provided an elevator, in addition to a rather gracious staircase.

Another gripe I have is that hotel bathrooms are often far from their restaurants. I don't like having to get up from my chair in a luxurious and comfortable setting to travel down a public corridor and through a lobby to find my destination. My feelings of well-being and comfort are lost. Last spring I stayed at The Westbury in London where the main bathrooms are downstairs, but luckily their restaurants have a small multisex facility, tactfully not designated "handicapped." Even The Ritz Restaurant in London no longer requires a gentleman (so designated because in order to dine there a coat and tie is required of him) to climb a steep set of stairs, since there is now a small facility easily accessible for one if not all, as long as he is suitably dressed.

The Ritz is most assuredly a classy hotel. Too often those who run classy hotels think it the height of refinement to place an attendant in the public toilet to help you manage your brief stay. There are so many things I need help with: motoring to the country, as I no longer drive a car; managing my finances; fixing my rebellious computer; typing this manuscript; even walking downstairs if there is no railing. I keep complaining about the Waldorf in Shanghai as they have no railing at the very first front step, and I feel foolish asking a doorman to assist me on my way to the Long Bar upstairs. Using the bathroom itself presents no problems. However, if it comes with an overeager attendant I never seem to have the proper single bill stuffed in my pocket, an omission that turns a non-event into anxiety-filled interlude. The worst part, when the proper amount cannot be found, is the guilt-ridden flight, head lowered, eyes straight ahead. Having attendants in bathrooms is not and never will be classy.

CHAPTER II

RESORTS

From Bermuda to Bali

When I was growing up our family didn't go to resorts. We went to a summer place, first on Cape Cod before the 1938 hurricane, and then in Keene Valley, south of Lake Placid in the Adirondacks. During spring vacation I would visit my aunt Marion, who rented a house each year on Point Shares near Hamilton, Bermuda. It was there that I first discovered resort hotels. Along with a couple of classmates I'd brought with me, we'd go searching for girls with whom we might spend an innocent evening. On our death-defying motorbikes we would cruise around, visiting the sprawling Elbow Beach Club, the Belmont, Castle Harbor, or, when the girls came from rich families, the Coral Beach Club. If the girls were Greek, we'd head for the

MANDARIN ORIENTAL, SANYA, IN CHINA.

Hamilton Princess, a much more formal and fancy resort reminiscent of The Pierre in New York where so many of them lived.

In 1953 when my aunt Ethel took John Loengard and me on an intense art and architecture trip in Europe, she gave us a break or two from our seriously educational tours with visits to a few resorts. No one could call her frivolous or picture her lounging on a beach in a bathing costume. But after we'd traveled from Genoa to Aosta, Courmayeur, Mantua, Milan, Bergamo, Padua, and more, and we had arrived in Venice she took us to the Lido where, of course, there is a famous beach. Our destination was not the super-deluxe Excelsior Palace—too fancy—but the first-class Grand Hotel Des Bains, built in 1900 a few blocks along the shore. Alas, few things stay the same. The Excelsior Palace, which we sneaked inside and explored, was the most marvelous Moorish confection imaginable, dating from 1908. It was later stripped of all its decoration and modernized beyond recognition. Only the ballroom escaped this destruction, but it is still worth viewing for a hint of what once was. The Grand Hotel Des Bains has become merely the Hotel Des Bains. It's been abandoned by its current owner Starwood and made into an apartment house. I was barely eighteen when I fell in love with this fin de siècle treasure, creaking wood floors, potted palms, and all. Years later Luchino Visconti restored its grandeur for his powerful film *Death in Venice,* based on Thomas Mann's novella. Dirk Bogarde played Gustav von Aschenbach, an older man who has come to the resort for health reasons and expires, with visions of the beautiful nubile boy Tadzio cavorting on the beach, to the haunting Adagietto from Gustav Mahler's Fifth Symphony.

My visit with Aunt Ethel and cousin John was considerably

less baroque but we appreciated the authentic period architecture, the beach, and—even more, I'm afraid—the enormous swimming pool, said to be the largest in Italy at the time. In years to come I was to give at its side many delicious and highly appreciated lunches for those members of the Save Venice Fund who otherwise would have been sweltering in town. Roman pines, shaded lawn, pasta and wine, straw hats, and convivial people were highlights of my entertaining efforts, happily remembered by me and I hope by all, including Ann Nitze and her son Charles, Alexis Gregory who first brought Georgie Abreu from Paris, Marife Hernandez, Shelley Schwarz, Marion Bedrick, the Esteves from San Paolo, the unforgettable, irrepressible Princess Cigi Ismeni, and many, many more. Although the Lido is an island, it's not a desert island. Staying in a hotel with no places to visit and stimulate the brain between occasional dips in the sea does not appeal to me, so having Venice a short motorboat ride away was a perfect solution to my resort-going needs. My sojourns there are sorely missed.

An ideal combination of resort and interesting city was Salvador in Bahia, Brazil. Although I've visited several colonial cities including Havana, which I went to once before and once after the revolution, none were as picturesque and architecturally fascinating as Salvador, where narrow cobblestone streets led up to more than seventy massive, breathtaking baroque churches. Less breathtaking was our first (and only) stay at a Club Med just off the coast. We did not mind paying for our drinks with beads strung around our necks; a caipirinha is a caipirinha no matter what your method of payment. However, the bizarre requirement that you must clap your hands and raise them above your head at the oddest times finally discouraged us. With "hands up!" still ringing in our ears, we fled.

At the Amandari in Bali there was no charming village nearby but there were so many steps to climb from the beach to your cottage that you would have been too exhausted for any cultural excursion. If you forgot your Agatha Christie in your room, you'd have to wait until much later to find out Poirot's conclusions on who done it (never the butler). Dining on the terrace was memorable, though—sublime at sunset, the architectural design refined.

I cannot conjure up any advice about resorts like Mana Kai in Hawaii or Caneel Bay in St. John. I have never stayed in either of those tropical paradises. I believe that my famous lack of inner resources would leave me feeling undernourished, not for food but intellectually; my mind would go blank. However, I have graced many wonderful resorts in the lovely towns along the Amalfi Coast and Bay of Naples. If my mind was going blank at the Cocumella in Sorrento, I could dash out to Pompeii or farther south, as I did last year, to the splendid temples at Paestum.

Designing a resort hotel today requires the creation of an environment very different from that of the old grand hotels. It is virtually a requirement now to have a view of the sea from the front entrance. All the guest rooms must also have a view, so they are constructed with long wings, strung out among the gardens and pools, not self-contained or monumental. The result is usually a long, long walk from the elevator, but the reward is a view of the Mediterranean or South China Sea. Since you usually don't have to go through the lobby to get to the pool or sea, you can keep your bathing suit on.

One characteristic of resort hotel guest rooms is that they are generally larger than those of in-town hotels. They also have a sitting area and often even a table for dining (this applies to fancy hotels, not the ones I stay in on Greek islands). Bathrooms are often bigger, too, especially those with an outside window, and in villa-like resorts they even have doors opening onto a patio. Individual swimming pools must be nice, although, and again sadly, I have never indulged in that extravagance myself.

My guest room in Jamaica one year was in a rented house, not a hotel. I did not spend an extra minute there, much less entertain friends in it. I definitely was not residing at Round Hill. I was staying with Alexis Gregory, and our party included Maria Theresa Train and her three lovely daughters. We were having Christmas dinner, enjoying a leg of lamb we'd smuggled onto the island in a golf bag, when two tremendously tall men came in, decidedly uninvited. Alexis thought they were commedia dell'arte performers and laughed heartily. My reaction was quite different. I removed my newly acquired Rolex, silver and gold, not ostentatiously all gold, and held it high above my head. They took my travelers' checks, too (that note dates my story), and although money was lost, no harm was done. In fact, after the incident Alexis's friends and I were entertained morning, noon, and night, so afraid were the local owners of the house that Alexis, who is very well connected, would tell lurid tales in New York, London, and Paris and property values would plummet. They did not, and I have returned several times but only to houses that boast a guard. My first Jamaican sojourn will not help you choose a suitable resort there, but it is very much part of my resort-going experience.

When it comes to finding a resort for relaxation, I have definite ideas. I'm not interested in a restful, desert island with nothing to look at but swaying palms and endless sandy beaches. In Mexico I once stayed with friends at Costa Careyes, an architecturally fabulous gated community in Jalisco that was not strictly speaking a hotel and where everything and everyone was so, so grand—with the possible exception of Sylvester Stallone who was *definitely* not part of our group. After a few days of such exclusivity, I longed to drive down the hill through those gates and visit the tiny village that was just visible from our hilltop enclave. I never did—no car, no native color, no guts. An otherwise delightful trip could have been so much more meaningful.

VISITING A NEARBY VILLAGE was no problem when I was staying at the Villa Feltrinelli, a hotel on the eastern shore of Lake Garda in northeast Italy. Ironically it had served as Mussolini's last refuge in exile. I could go on for paragraphs on how superb this hotel is, the perfection of every aspect of the rooms (they have a button you can push to hear full-length opera, not excerpts, sung by the likes of Domingo and Price), the restaurant, the gardens, the understated, tastefully simple, elegant swimming pool, all conceived and developed by Bob Burns who had extended his visionary touch from China, Japan, Hawaii, and New York finally to Lake Garda. Staying at the Villa Feltrinelli, you are hardly isolated. The house D'Annunzio shared with Ellen Terry is interesting to visit, and Verona is not far away.

VILLA FELTRINELLI, LAKE GARDA, ITALY.
Perfect in all ways, thanks to its creator Bob Burns.

But more important to me is the small "fishing village" not a mile from the hotel's entrance where along the shore there are several charming trattorias offering you a chilled Pinot Grigio with your prosciutto and melon and a sturdy Chianti with your spaghetti al pomodoro. The trattorias provide more than a nice contrast with the refined food served on the terrace of the elegant Villa Feltrinelli. *The best of both worlds* is my idea of a perfect resort experience, and Villa Feltrinelli is ideally located to provide it.

CHAPTER 12

HOTEL POOLS

For Swimming or for Socializing

THE RITZ IN LONDON DOES NOT HAVE A pool; nor can one imagine Mr. Ritz himself doing morning laps before taking his very English breakfast in the hotel's glorious Ritz Restaurant on Green Park or, more likely, in his vast suite upstairs. On the other hand the Ritz in Paris has a very elaborate pool in its basement, an inelegant word for the space where it is housed. Because the pool is below ground the owners decided years ago to demolish the perfectly proportioned, classically grand restaurant L'Espadon, which is on the garden level directly above, to create a skylight for the lap swimmers below. Letters were written by me and others far more influential, and that lovely restaurant was

FOUR SEASONS HOTEL HONG KONG.

saved. Incidentally, if you insist on having a swimming pool with natural light when you're staying at a grand hotel in Paris, you'll find one on the roof of the Bristol. Its modest size does not make it suitable for laps. Not a problem for me, but for others, perhaps.

A swimming pool is included in the design of most hotels simple or grand. In five-star properties the pools are generally Olympic-sized or larger. Outdoor pools may be spread over acres, particularly in China where their popularity is enhanced by the fact that they are often partially shaded. The Chinese do not like to be exposed to the sun, so their pools and beaches tend to be populated by Westerners thrilled to have their skin darkened and seemingly oblivious to the fact that wrinkles will inevitably follow—or worse. Chinese outdoor pools often start outside a hotel's main lobby and wind around, coming out next to the guest room wing. It can be unsettling when you're lounging on the balcony of your first-floor room at the Hainan Island Ritz-Carlton by the South China Sea, sipping a glass of chilled white wine from the minibar, and suddenly a large, decidedly un-buff male floats by on a raft.

The kind of pools I prefer are not Olympic in size and do not snake around next to my private balcony. Laps may be done, but only in the early morning; the rest of the time people gather around the edge, gossiping, reading, and, most happily, lunching. I would categorize these pools as social. The most famous social pool is at The Beverly Hills Hotel. I haven't stayed there often, but it's been long enough to hear the loudspeaker call out that Mr. Goldwyn or Miss Gardner was wanted on something then called the telephone.

Only slightly less well known is the pool at the Cipriani in

Venice, which I recall as very social indeed. The island is extremely hot in the summer and remains so during the first week in September, aka "Holy Week" to signify the descent of assorted socialites on that pearl of the Adriatic with more than a few pearls and diamonds stuffed in their Louis Vuitton suitcases. Among the brightly colored caftans, jauntily cocked straw hats, and half-sipped Bellinis, one heartfelt moment stands apart from the usual tra la la. One evening I was seated next to medical research pioneer and fashion icon Deeda Blair at an extremely posh dinner given by Annette de la Renta and Jayne Wrightsman at The Gritti (I was asked as a poor relation to one of Annette's best friends, but still). I asked Deeda what she was doing. Two hours went by, during which time I hardly turned to my other dinner partner, so enthralled was I by her description of the medical lifesaving wonders she and Maurice Tempelsman were creating at the Harvard AIDS Initiative. I was both impressed and moved. Having volunteered and raised money for an AIDS organization myself, I sent a check to her room that night. The next morning as I strolled around the Cipriani pool, Deeda's lovely face popped out of the water and she said, "Instant gratification!" It was a gratifying moment for me indeed among all those caftans and straw hats.

"Holy Week" is also the week of the Venice Film Festival, held on the Lido across the lagoon. One September I went with my daughter, my then son-in-law, and their ravishingly adorable year-old daughter Nuala. That one turned heads, especially Tom Cruise's and Nicole Kidman's, in town for the film festival. We collided with them as we all tried to get through the narrow revolving door at Harry's Bar. Knowing they were childless, did I detect a slight look of envy from those two equally beautiful

HOTEL CIPRIANI, VENICE.
No hat is finer than Nan Kempner's.

stars? At Harry's Bar it was essential to be seated downstairs; up the stairs you would be chilled from the cold winds of Siberia. The beautiful couples were of course downstairs, but then so was the beautiful baby, in the best corner table, thank you.

My numerous trips to Venice were not always about securing one of the best tables downstairs at Harry's Bar. Thanks to the directors of Save Venice, Larry Lovett and Bea and Bob Guthrie—and after a falling-out, Khalil Rizk and Alexis Gregory, founder of the excellent competing charity Venetian Heritage—my trips were more than memorable. I was privileged to visit and dine in Venice's most famous and fabulous private palazzi and Palladian villas, where I sipped champagne in their gardens and danced in their ballrooms. I was exposed to great works of art seldom seen by the public, including two magnificent oversized statues by

HOTEL CIPRIANI, VENICE.
The pool is an important reason to stay here, more for socializing than for swimming.

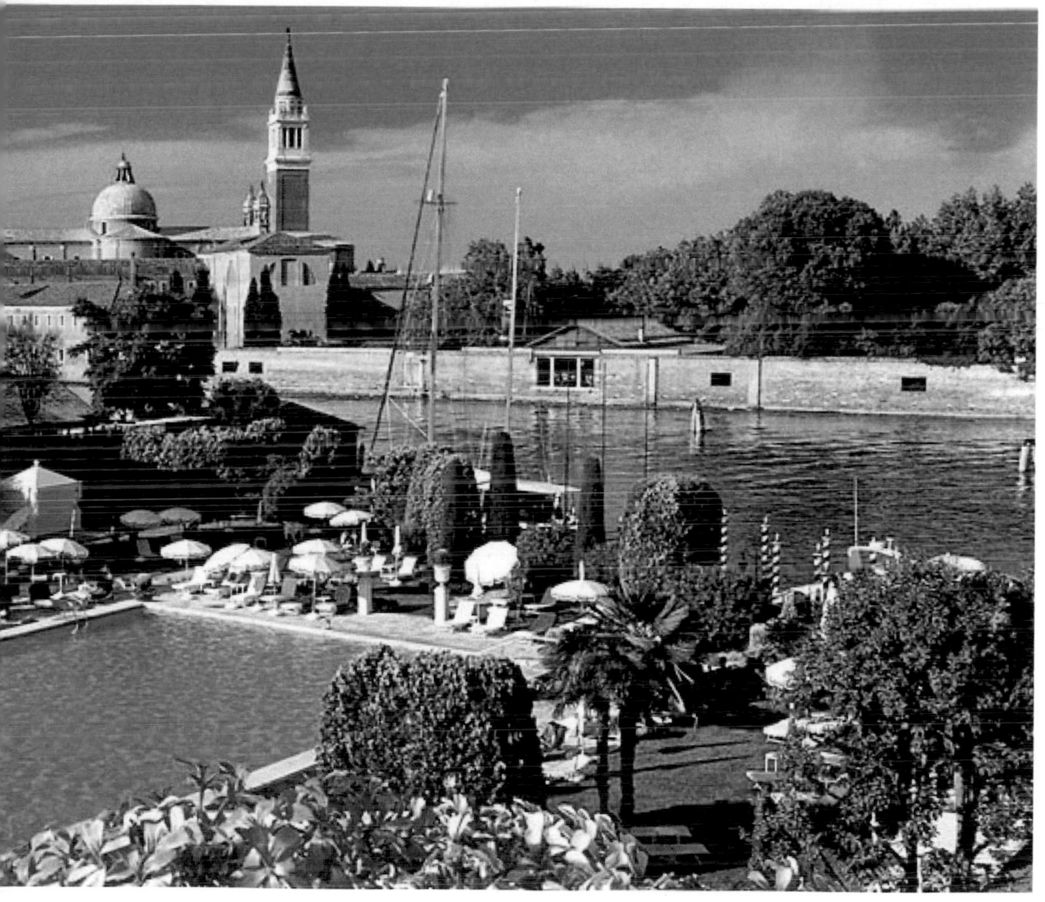

Canova owned by the Marchese Alberto Berlingieri that were locked away in a modest third-floor room in the Grand Canal palazzo next to the Hotel Europa. Private concerts were held in spaces closed to the public: the cloisters of the church of San Giorgio and the San Marco Basilica.

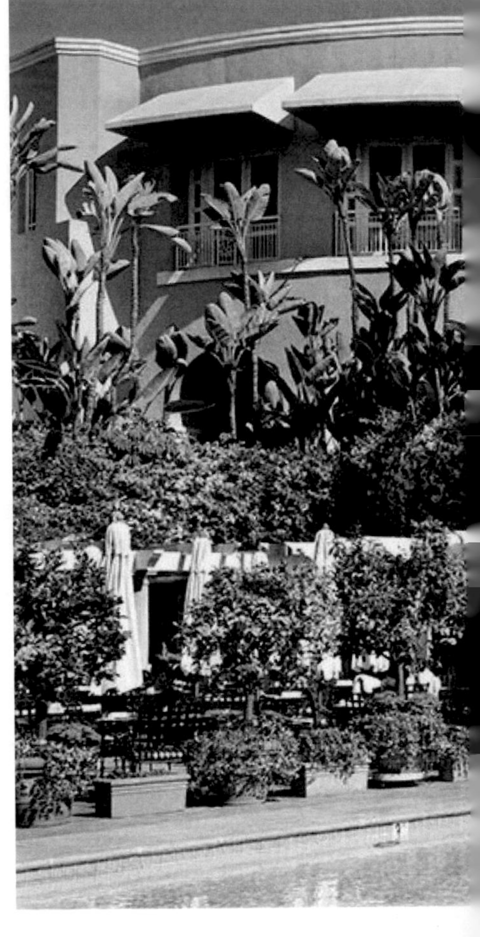

Loving art as I do, I remember gazing rapturously at the Veronese frescoes in the Palladian Villa di Maser, where I learned to keep my priorities straight. The Venetian school of painting is almost my favorite, so naturally I was enthralled to see them. Too enthralled, perhaps, as soon I found myself to be the only person left inside the villa. All the others, again in their straw hats, were out in the garden organizing tables and jostling to join the best places next to friends or people whom they wished were friends. There were only two chairs, far from the center, left for me. Good placement trumps an extra few minutes of art appreciation, even in Venice. Well, especially in Venice.

While the glamour of social pools is largely due to the people who lounge around them, the glamour of a rooftop pool may be in the setting. The Park Hyatt Tokyo pool, seen in the movie *Lost in Translation*, looks over that vast city, as does the hotel's health club, including the treadmill that boasted even me a couple

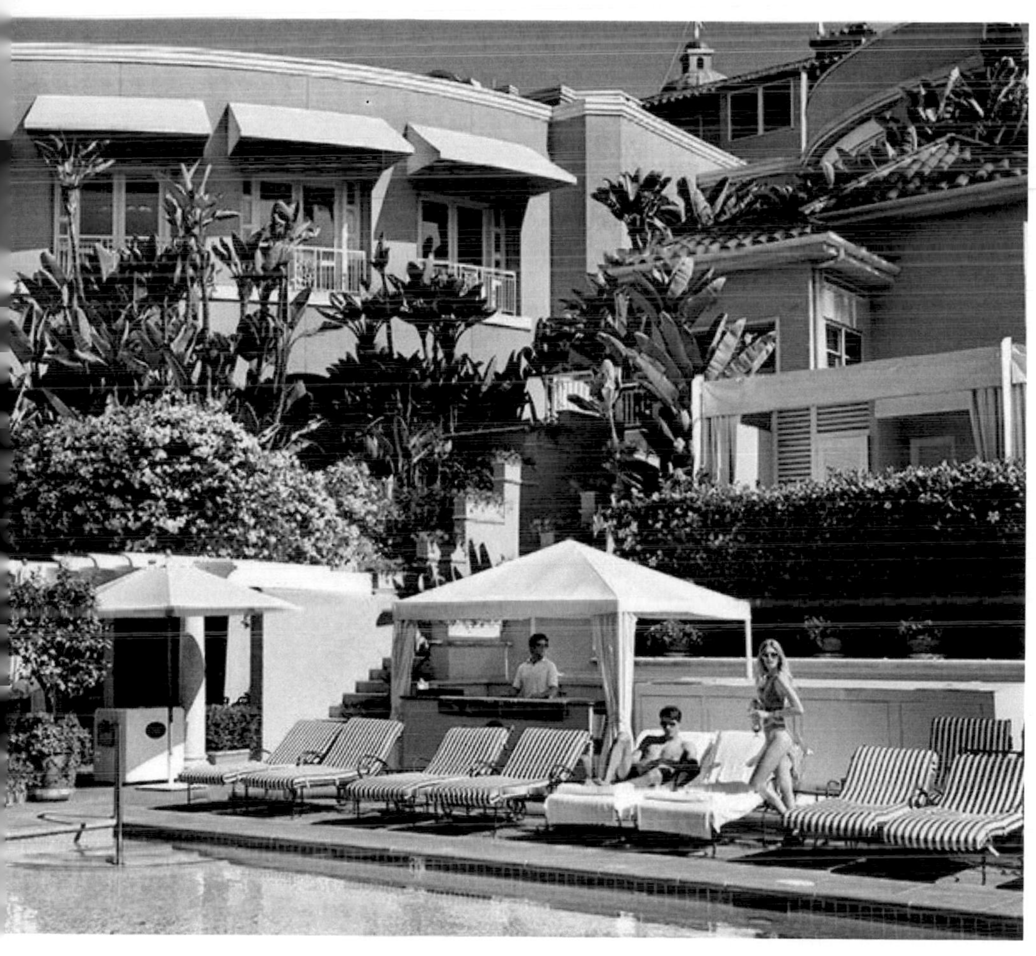

THE BEVERLY HILLS HOTEL.
Stars were once paged by loudspeaker here,
but they now rely on cellphones.

of times as I tried to stay healthy on a business trip. Tokyo is not my favorite city, so seeing it from above is not particularly special for me. Hong Kong, on the other hand, is one of my favorites, and the views from the rooftop pool at the Peninsula over the harbor to the skyscrapers that reach almost to the peak are dazzling.

Less dazzling is the question of what you do about children enjoying their playtime in these glamorous settings. By children, I really mean young boys who for reasons unknown can never get enough of hurtling themselves into the water, getting out, and immediately jumping in again and again and again, drenching the people sitting nearby. In Athens, a city that is even hotter in the summer than Venice, the developer of the Hilton, which was built in 1960, had the foresight to include a really large swimming pool, a blessing after you've trudged up to the Acropolis and back through Athens's labyrinthine historical neighborhood Pláka. Years back, I was relaxing by the pool around three o'clock, siesta time for all Athenians. I would have been enjoying an hour or two of peace except that an American family, three boys and their father, was also at the pool. The boys were doing what boys will do, playing in and out of the water thunderously while their father looked on approvingly. As a New Yorker, I am well practiced at confronting rudeness on the Number Six Lexington Avenue subway line, and I soon scorned them into silence.

At the Lyford Cay Club in Nassau I discovered that young boys are not allowed to wear baseball caps on backward—no hip-hopping allowed at Lyford! They are also discouraged from jumping in and out of the swimming pool. I have no idea how successfully the first edict is being adhered to because my first and only visit there was out of season. Apparently the second edict was being ignored. I had been brought to the club on a professional basis to see if I could find a location for a child-oriented pool. It was never built, being too expensive. Nevertheless, I think separate pools are the answer, and a few Asian clients have requested them.

Although I have been to very few saltwater pools, I love them. When I'm in a regular pool, one short dunk to cool off does it for me. In a saltwater pool I paddle and swim underwater, as I do in the ocean. When I get out I tingle with a feeling of well-being. I recently stayed at Hostal de la Gavina, a sprawling low-rise resort far north of Barcelona, which has a large saltwater pool overlooking the sea and a rather unappealing beach quite a way below. I wish more hotels with limited access to beaches, like this one, would include saltwater pools.

The mere mention of pools filled with salt water reminds me of the very special times five years running I was a guest of the charming Doda Voridis at her spacious Mediterranean-style villa in Porto Rafti, by the sea near Cape Sounion. I will not run through the names of the other guests as that would exceed my quota of name-dropping, but I will say that Kenny Lane was part of our group.

The saltwater pool set high above the sea was the center of the day's activities, from our early-morning dips, coffee served with *The New York Times*, to lunch in the pavilion followed by a siesta once the gossip had died down. The pool and adjoining lawn were the setting for a gala seated dinner for almost one hundred locals, plus a smattering of visitors from nearby yachts. Lots of dancing to Greek music, lots of bouzouki playing. Festive. The entire hill above the pool was lit up, illuminating hundreds of bushes and thousands of flowers. As the region of Attica is very arid, one had to assume that a virtual army had been amassed to water them. A magical time, a magical saltwater pool. Hotel operators, are you taking note? You need not include the bouzouki playing along with the salt, unless you are so inclined.

I've made a couple of mildly disparaging references to lap swimmers in this book so it will come as no surprise to learn that I'm not a great swimmer myself. But there are a few hotel pools for which I have traveled far, and paid dearly, in order to enjoy a leisurely paddle in placid waters. One of the most beautiful outdoor pools I know is at the Mandarin Oriental, Sanya on Hainan Island. Actually there are three. The first is on top near the guest rooms, although not so near that a floating body will drift by your balcony as it may at the Ritz-Carlton a few miles away. This pool is very natural, jungle-like and tropical. The one below is more architectural, and the one by the beach more formal: lovely, less intricate, but romantic. One's South China Sea pool fantasies are realized.

As different as possible is the indoor pool, also in China, at the Fuchun Resort, a twenty-five-minute drive from Hangzhou and its West Lake, one of the country's most famous beauty spots. Perhaps you don't think of China and golf together, but the sport is very popular with the newly very rich. At Fuchun the players drive their balls between towering tea plants beside the small but lovely lake. Fuchun is not St. Andrew's in Scotland and therefore hardly likely to attract my golf-obsessed friends, and it's certainly not around the corner, either, but it is beautiful. The indoor pool at the hotel is a perfect square, almost as tall as it is wide, and it's hushed

THE PENINSULA SHANGHAI.
Laps are swum under the skylight, though not by me.

since all the guests are out on the golf course among those tea plants. The ceiling is supported by elaborate wood tresses with two slanting sides that have low doors, letting the light in discreetly. Temple-like, serene, and lovely.

My absolute favorite hotel pool is not serene, not in a jungle, not especially social, not by the sea, nor at the top of a tower. It consists of two pools, closely connected, on the sixth floor of the

Four Seasons in the aptly named district of Central. They overlook the Hong Kong harbor and the rapidly growing skyline of Kowloon beyond. Before I extol these pools' virtues, I must confess that the entrance to the pool and spa complex breaks every hotel design rule imaginable. The small foyer is also the entrance to the hotel's sumptuous Caprice, which is, as I've mentioned, the city's most glittering restaurant, with many chandeliers, crimson banquettes, and a floor lit from below. Fancy, fancy, and the locals who dine here dress appropriately even at lunch, a rare gesture in this dressed-down world. No one seems to care that these properly attired diners share the foyer with the bathing suit set whose bodies, one can only hope, are at least covered by the hotel's generous Frette robes. At BBG we would have considered this design a planning disaster but because both destinations are so gorgeous, all is forgiven.

All rules can be broken as long as they are broken with real style. Entering the pools several floors up, you see a vast expanse of water and at its infinity edge, of course, the harbor and the towers in Kowloon. After a day's work or play it is the most glamorous setting imaginable in which to relax and cool off from Hong Kong's often hot and humid days. Even in the middle of the winter I have swum in those pools, diving down in the comfortably heated water to find that Christmas carols were audible below the surface. Listening to Bing Crosby sing "White Christmas" underwater is a very Hong Kong Christmas experience in a city that celebrates that holiday so extravagantly. Every lofty hotel lobby and shopping mall court has the largest, most lavishly decorated Christmas tree. Santa Clauses, sleighs, and reindeers skitter up the façades of office buildings, outlined by colored lights. Holiday efforts on Park and Fifth avenues seem underwhelming when compared with Hong Kong's over-the-top decorations and outdoor pools that play Christmas carols beneath the water. Where's our Christmas spirit next to that of the Chinese? They even greet you with "Merry Christmas" instead of the one-size-fits-all "Happy Holidays," a salutation that I find insipid, as does our current president, probably our only area of agreement.

After experiencing the extraordinary hotel pools I've described it is difficult for me to find much enthusiasm for donning my robe and slippers and going downstairs for a dip in the one belonging to a Holiday Inn, this time near the Jacksonville airport, located beside a parking lot. In terms of hotel pools I have been spoiled rotten.

CHAPTER 13

SPAS AND GYMS

For Some, the Important Thing

"HOW MANY TIMES A WEEK DO YOU GO to your health club"? I can't remember ever being asked that question in the 1960s and 1970s. When I lived at 131 East Sixty-Sixth Street, I never left my landmarked apartment building to trudge over to Third Avenue—or worse yet Second—and disappear into an overlit basement to run on a treadmill or lift a weight. My answer would have been, "Never." Can you imagine behaving that way these days? Perhaps you have a serious heart condition or you keep a stationary bike in your bedroom. If my Park and Fifth avenue friends are asked that question they inevita-

TREATMENT ROOM AT THE PENINSULA HOTEL NEW YORK

bly reply that they have a gym in their building so they do not have to go to a health club, or a marvelous trainer comes to *them* two or three times a week. Nowadays most of us, it seems, talk of little else but staying healthy, apparently hoping to live to 105 and have the *Sunday Times* report that we died "peacefully at home."

When I was planning InterContinentals and Sheratons all over the world, I remember including in the basement a small exercise room and a place to change and wash up. In renovations at the St. Regis we placed such a gym in the basement between a gift shop and the barbershop. The latter was considerably larger than the sports facility. To access this gym you had to parade through the lobby to the handicapped elevator or share a stairway with people going to the business and party rooms. No need to wear a bathrobe—there wasn't a pool. Staying healthy was not aided by the facilities at the St. Regis.

Now we plan hotel health clubs and spas as big as thirty thousand square feet. These facilities have left the basement and are given prime locations. Spa treatment rooms have windows facing into gardens. These treatment rooms are always private, allowing you to be pulled and pampered in open air surrounded by flowers, bushes, and trees. No longer a cubicle, each room has at least a private shower and a massage table surrounded by ample space, so much so that spas provide deluxe rooms with two tables for his and hers, or his and his, or whatever. The exercise rooms are enormous, the nearby pool never less than Olympic-sized. One thing I do not like is having the exercise room with its stationary bikes visible from the pool, which is often the case today. I still think of hotel pools in terms of recreation, of chatting there with a Bellini in hand as I did in my days at the Cipriani. I cannot bly reply that they have a gym in their building so they do not have to go to a health club, or a marvelous trainer comes to *them* two or three times a week. Nowadays most of us, it seems, talk of little else but staying healthy, apparently hoping to live to 105 and have the *Sunday Times* report that we died "peacefully at home."

When I was planning InterContinentals and Sheratons all over the world, I remember including in the basement a small exercise room and a place to change and wash up. In renovations at the St. Regis we placed such a gym in the basement between a gift shop and the barbershop. The latter was considerably larger than the sports facility. To access this gym you had to parade through the lobby to the handicapped elevator or share a stairway with people going to the business and party rooms. No need to wear a bathrobe—there wasn't a pool. Staying healthy was not aided by the facilities at the St. Regis.

Now we plan hotel health clubs and spas as big as thirty thousand square feet. These facilities have left the basement and are given prime locations. Spa treatment rooms have windows facing into gardens. These treatment rooms are always private, allowing you to be pulled and pampered in open air surrounded by flowers, bushes, and trees. No longer a cubicle, each room has at least a private shower and a massage table surrounded by ample space, so much so that spas provide deluxe rooms with two tables for his and hers, or his and his, or whatever. The exercise rooms are enormous, the nearby pool never less than Olympic-sized. One thing I do not like is having the exercise room with its stationary bikes visible from the pool, which is often the case today. I still think of hotel pools in terms of recreation, of chatting there with a Bellini in hand as I did in my days at the Cipriani. I cannot visualize my ladies in caftans and straw hats gaping at a person in Nike gym shorts pumping away on a stationary bike.

As I have written, people choose hotels for their location, their special features, their ambience, and, of course, the price of their rooms. More and more my friends are also looking for the best gym and spa facilities. Super designer Mary McFadden once asked me for a hotel recommendation in Taipei, Taiwan. I thought a hotel like the Hyatt Regency would be too glitzy for Mary, who was invariably elegant, even in simple tennis whites. I suggested a place where I thought she would be happy, my own choice, the tasteful if somewhat conservative Sherwood Taipei. She immediately inquired about the gym. Total blank. She chose the Hyatt Regency, glitz be damned.

Taking the health aspect even further, hotels are being named not the Grand or the Excelsior, but for their lavish health clubs and spas. Several Equinox hotels have opened and I assume they are successful, but their success will not be celebrated by me. Kale salad in the restaurant, carrot juice in the bar?

Hudson Yards developer Steve Ross is building his mega city on the far West Side to include several office towers, apartment buildings, high-end stores and convenience ones, as well as a large open green space graced by a multistory staircase-themed sculpture. The complex will include just one hotel, with a spectacular spa theme. As there are few other habitable hotels in this part of the city, it is an interesting choice—but to me a controversial one. Since Ross's Related Companies business is always successful I am sure this venture will be, too. "Waiter, can you please add a little more vodka to my carrotini?" I think I would prefer to stay at the Carlyle.

I, who have been upgraded to the most sumptuous suites and dined in the grandest of grand dining rooms, am sorely underprivileged in that I had never before actually treated myself to a super hotel spa experience. A massage in a woodshed behind the Des Bains pool and two relaxing sessions in a dingy dark room in Shanghai hardly count. As a research project supported by my editor friend Maggie Simmons, I reluctantly booked a two-hour session at the Peninsula Spa in New York. Maggie was not giving me this treatment as an early Christmas present, something I later regretted when I came to pay the bill. Never mind, I felt wonderful afterward and might consider giving up three or four lunches at La Grenouille in order to savor that feeling again.

At the Peninsula Spa, I was feeling slightly nervous but was met at the reception by a charming woman in black, who greeted me enthusiastically. She handed me over to a young man who gave me a brief tour of the facilities, including the locker rooms and relaxation room. He also asked me whether I preferred a woman or man. A man please, me being me. I asked just one question: Was the tip included in the bill? Remembering my few times in the shack behind the pool at the Des Bains in Venice, I knew that for the last fifteen minutes I would be worrying about how much to tip my masseur instead of enjoying his rather deft manipulation of what pass for muscles on my anything-but-robust frame. Anyway I was introduced to my physical therapist and masseur Jody, who was young and personable and asked if I wanted the hot jade rock treatment. It sounded painful but as I did not want to seem cowardly I meekly murmured in the affirmative. The next and only other question asked was what kind of music would I like. It did not seem like a good time finally to

DUKES HOTEL

learn to appreciate the score of *Hamilton*, so I answered, "Classical, please," as I had recently found that a Beethoven piano concerto works quite well to settle the nerves during an MRI. What I got was a sort of soothing pseudo-Oriental elevator music that suited perfectly my hushed, soporific surroundings.

I will not give you a blow-by-blow description of my treatment except that it felt lovely. The hot jade rocks were mercifully applied gently and I felt relaxed and suitably radiant after. I left properly, telling Jody that I would be seeing him soon although I'm afraid a return visit is unlikely. Ultimately I have decided that I love my lunches at La Grenouille much too much.

Although fancy spas may never become an essential part of my life, self-preservation remains and I go to my simple, no-frills health club around the corner four times a week, I might say almost religiously: twice on a stationary bicycle, twice with my marvelous trainer, Michael Olivieri. I have little wish to live to be 105, but a bit past 85 would be nice.

CHAPTER 14

BOUTIQUE HOTELS

Enjoy the Charm, Ignore the Attitude

IN THE OLD DAYS, A SMALL CHARMING HOTEL was a small charming hotel with full service. It had all the assets of a much larger hotel such as a restaurant, a bar, often a library, and even a couple of small meeting rooms. The guest rooms were often singles. Nevertheless, people lucky enough to book into one of these small hotels would not trade them for the Ritz. I must admit that I have many well-heeled friends who wouldn't go to London if they had to stay at the Stafford. While the guest rooms are charming, they're almost as expensive as those at the Ritz though they are considerably smaller. As Terry

DUKES HOTEL, LONDON.

Holmes, the then general manager of both hotels, said to me, "Those who are trying to make it, stay at the Ritz; those who have made it, stay at the Stafford." I was not surprised to see Mary and Howdy Phipps emerging from the front door one morning, both swearing that they would not dream of staying anywhere else. Dukes Hotel, around the corner with smaller rooms, is almost as charming and nearly as expensive.

Both these hotels are very popular with those people who prize intimacy, charm, and friendly, attentive service. Both have delightful cozy bars, although the American sports theme at the Stafford turns me off a bit, again, me being me. I prefer Dukes's bar, even though it is much smaller, because the bartender serves the best martinis in London. They are delicious and without a doubt the most costly. Fame has its price.

I have already mentioned how much I had liked the France et Choiseul in Paris, with its friendly, personal service, before it became Costes, a boutique hotel. The service is now somewhat cold and loaded with attitude. The hotel has very trendy furniture, and the effect downstairs is admittedly stunning, especially in the dining room. Another change is the price, which has skyrocketed. Nevertheless, boutique hotels are not necessarily more expensive than other small hotels.

My encounters with boutique hotels, especially those that are categorized as hip, have been erratic. At the St. Martins Lane Hotel in London, the hippest of hip, I was discouraged from having a drink in the bar even though I was appropriately dressed, having just visited Brooks's, a venerable men's club, on my way to the theater. Obviously I was too appropriately dressed from the point of view of the men in black at front door. My request to visit the bar was greeted by haughty smirks. Discouraged, I went on my way. In Amsterdam I was similarly shunned when I asked for a drink in the bar at Blakes. I can wear black just as well as the next one but I am not about to bring a special black look to Europe simply in order to be welcomed by those disdainful young men. Even when I dressed in black, they would see my wrinkles and decide that I had wandered into the wrong hotel. I realize that it is churlish of me but I am not inclined to write about hotels where I do not feel comfortable or welcomed. Sorry to say, hip I am not.

The only person I hate to discuss as much as Donald Trump is Kim Kardashian. However, an incident involving the theft of ten million dollars of her jewelry brings me to make a point about staying in boutique hotels. No matter how luxurious they may be, they have a drawback that would never have occurred to me, or indeed anyone accustomed to trailing a carry-on suitcase into their guest room. My bag would be of no interest to a thief; instead of diamond bracelets it is packed with pills and eye drops for glaucoma. But if you are carrying around expensive jewels you should be aware that a small, exclusive residential hotel does not have the security guaranteed at a larger luxury hotel such as a Mandarin Oriental, a Peninsula, or even a Ritz. If you're curious about the name of the hotel where Ms. Kardashian's robbery took place, I can tell you that I combed *The New York Times* to find it. Hôtel de Pourtalès. Never heard of the place? Neither had I.

Having peevishly dismissed all trendy boutique hotels on the grounds that those men in black behind the front desk possess what is usually described as "an attitude," last winter while in Los Angeles I chose not to stay at my former usual haunt, The Penin-

HÔTEL COSTES, PARIS.
Charming indeed, and only occasionally marred by a staff member's attitude.

sula Beverly Hills, but instead to try The Standard (almost in actual Hollywood) to be closer to my granddaughter. She lives smack on the Walk of Fame, which borders Hollywood Boulevard. She is not that near to the center, Grauman's Chinese Theatre, and the star in the pavement outside her front door is the one that commemorates Ona Munson (Belle Watkins in *Gone with the Wind*), not Bette Davis or even Julia Roberts. To be close to all this history and my granddaughter was the reason I chose The Standard.

Almost immediately—from the first cheery greeting at the front door to my view of the largish pool surrounded by the most striking blue AstroTurf (of all things) from my south-facing uncluttered corner room, which had two balconies and a large stall shower without a trace of an extraneous bathtub—I was charmed. Furthermore, apparently

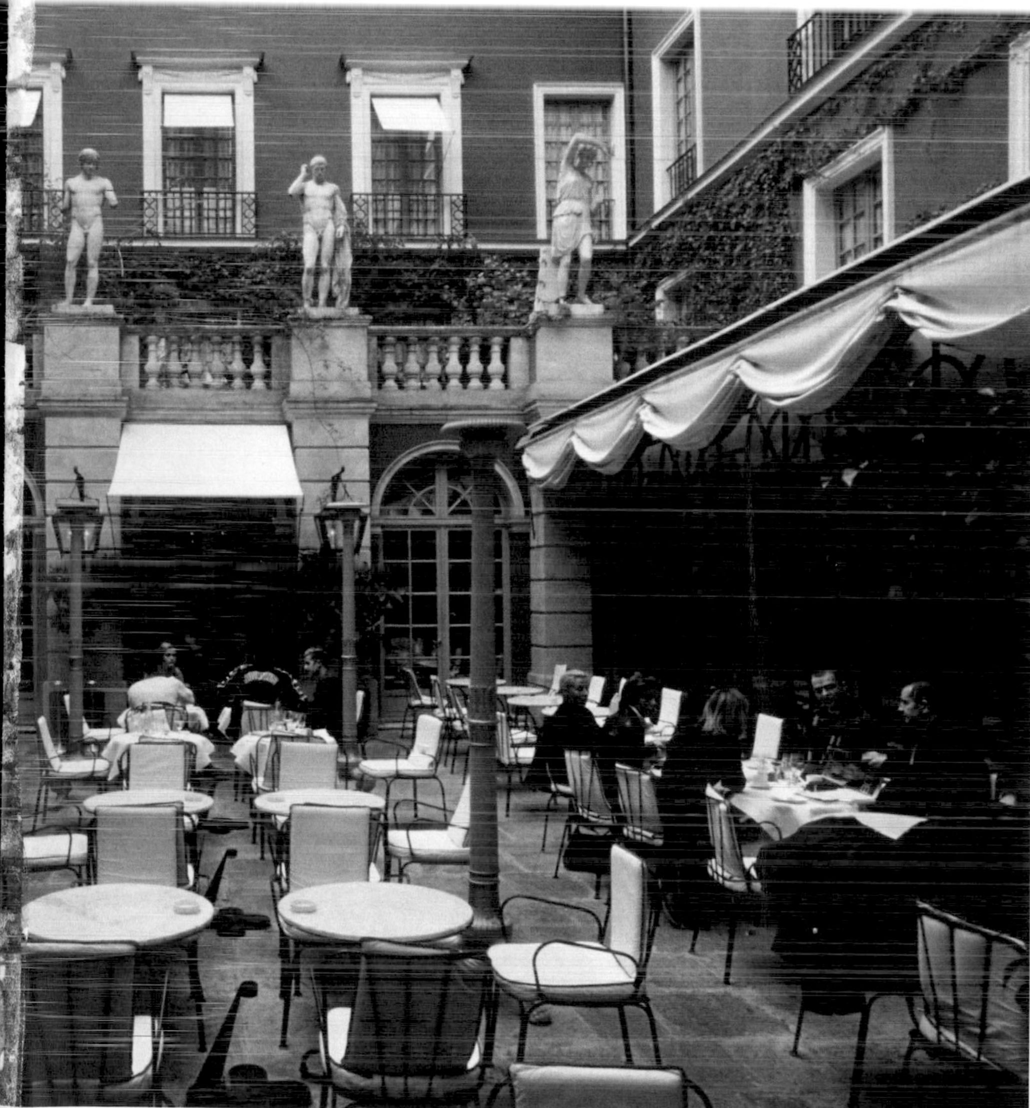

merry millennials do not celebrate Christmas in trendy hotels. The Standard was nearly empty, sparing me beer-guzzling poolside parties.

Location is always important to non-driving me. The hotel on Sunset Boulevard is happily almost across from the legend-

THE STANDARD, HOLLYWOOD.

My family and Tyree recently celebrated a very unwhite Christmas here.

ary Chateau Marmont. Most important, the jeans-wearing, occasionally shorts-sporting staff was devoid of attitude, and adorable. They were also suitably Christmassy in a town that boasted nary a decorated tree. The sight of the one meager string of lights hung behind the bar at the otherwise simple Mexican joint on the other side of Sunset did not do much to lift my spirits. Unlike Irving Berlin caught at The Beverly Hills Hotel over the holidays in 1943, I was not "Dreaming of a White Christmas." For a brief moment, sipping my margarita at a bar that bordered on being seasonably sleazy, I thought of the times in the Four Seasons Hong Kong when I heard Bing Crosby sing that anthem underwater in the pool. Both in Old Hollywood and new Hong Kong my Christmases were certainly not "like the ones I used to know."

CHPATER 15

CASINOS

More than Roulette

IN LIFE I HAVE NOT TAKEN MANY CHANCES. Too often I have played it safe. When the office pool for the Super Bowl is announced each year I do not put myself down for a square. I do not spend time playing roulette in casinos, whether I am in Las Vegas, Atlantic City, or Monte Carlo for that matter. My introduction to casino hotels was far from auspicious.

When I was studying at the Harvard Graduate School of Design students were encouraged to take a summer job in a construction company. Looking at fairly frail me you might not have hired me to be a carpenter, but hired I was, to bang twelve-penny nails into floorboards all summer long under a brilliant Atherton sun down on the peninsula, south of San Francisco.

BELLAGIO LAS VEGAS.

Feeling that I deserved a break from my labors I took a bus trip to the Grand Canyon with a stopover in Las Vegas to survey its then famous hotels: Wilbur Clark's Desert Inn, the Flamingo, the Sands, the Tropicana, the Riviera, the New Frontier, and even the lowest of the low, the Thunderbird. Outside several I would find a far-off deck chair and wiggle out of my clothes, leaving me in my bathing suit ready to plunge into the pool. Every attempt was thwarted by an unsympathetic guard, even at the Thunderbird, so I had to continue to Flagstaff on a Greyhound bus unrefreshed. On recent trips I have booked a room and thus been able to enjoy the elaborate pool areas of the Bellagio, the Venetian, the Wynn, and most recently the understated but typically classy Four Seasons, a hotel so un-glitzy that you would not know, for better or worse, that you were in Las Vegas.

In the old days casino hotels were designed so that no daylight was allowed to penetrate the severe darkness of the public floors, encouraging people to huddle over the slot machines day and night, forgetting their mothers' admonishments that if it is a beautiful day they must go out and play in the sunshine, usually to kick a ball. My mother was no different in directing me into the sunshine but she knew better than to add the bit about balls, knowing that I did not readily play with them, even if they were tennis balls.

Today's casino hotels aim for a far more varied clientele than hard-core gamblers. Their lobbies swarm with frolicking convention-goers, and families complete with strollers and porta-cribs. You still have to travel through or at least pass by the casino to get from the front desk to the elevators, restaurants, bars, nightclubs, shops, and pool bars. The Bellagio conceived by

THE MARLBOROUGH-BLENHEIM, ATLANTIC CITY.
At this hotel (now gone), fabulous fantasy gave way to mediocrity.

Steve Wynn was the first giant complex to flood the check-in lobby with daylight and to add two gardens, one behind the front desk. I would prefer that it did not have dozens of Dale Chihuly glass sculptures dangling from the ceiling, a flagrant example of decorative excess. Still, Las Vegas is all about excess, so why not? I'd rather see this undeniably famous sculptor's work there even by the dozens than the out-of-character creation that hangs aggressively in Claridge's elegant lobby in London. Relevance has its place.

Old and New Bond streets have every conceivable luxury store from Paris, Milan, and New York, but the hotel shopping areas in Las Vegas have almost as many. In some cases, like the Bellagio and Wynn, they are housed in delightful, sun-filled

My fantasy-filled renovation of the Ritz hotel in Atlantic City, for Warner LeRoy, was never built.

The Ritz that was built, later torn down.

vaulted arcades. Delightful, yes, but not so enticing that I would be tempted to stop and buy a Hermès tie or, heaven forbid, a pair of Gucci loafers. Come to think of it, I can't remember having ever seen in any of these hotels a Zara or a Uniqlo, my haberdashers of choice these days. I have to admit that such stores might seem out of place on the Grand Canal or St. Mark's Square or in Sheldon Adelson's version of them at the Venetian. I feel a little guilty enjoying these pastiches of the real thing, having spent so much time on the Gritti Palace terrace on the real canal and at Caffè Florian on St. Mark's Square. My guilt is compounded by the fact that even one glass of white wine adds the tiniest amount to the coffers of that particular gentleman.

Here I may sound a bit like an expectant bride left at the altar by an uncaring cad, and that pretty much describes my relationship with the diminutive tycoon. After building the wildly successful Venetian he asked me to design an adjoining addition, the Palazzo, with more lavish rooms and suites, plus acres of public space where I could apply my long familiarity with the real Venice. My design would be not only authentic but also whimsical and fun. My work was heartfelt, but it did not quicken the tycoon's pulse. No job, no money, no future invitation to join him and the forty-fifth president at Mar-a-Lago.

It might be interesting to note that before anyone associated Mar-a-Lago with Donald Trump, one of my early assignments at Welton Becket was designing two projects for the future president. One was an apartment tower on Madison Avenue and Fifty-Ninth Street and the other a large addition to the old Bank of New York on Wall Street. As for the apartment tower, he and his then wife Ivana thought it would be the height of chic to place an outside elevator on the primary corner, depriving the project of its most valuable space. I noted that most people would not go up fifty floors in a glass contraption without having a shot of vodka first at The Plaza, which the Trumps then owned (still not a reason to sacrifice the space). Both could not have been more gracious in our meeting for three held in their smallish office across from Trump Tower. He lost both projects to others, hardly a display of his artful dealings.

Well over twenty years ago I visited Las Vegas to receive an honor bestowed on me by *Hospitality Design* magazine for my contribution to the industry. I stayed at the Sands just before it was torn down to make way for the Bellagio and I have on my refrigerator door magnets depicting works by Michelangelo, Bernini, and Wren, a small replica of that long-lost architectural gem. I do not remember my guest room at the Sands, but I am certain it was not grand. I resist giving Adelson credit, but he did build the first supersized guest room when he constructed the Venetian. The room was well over six hundred square feet with a sleeping area, a dropped living room, and a large bathroom containing a vanity with two sinks and a stall shower, all standard now for luxury properties but new at the time for Las Vegas. On my recent visit, again organized by *Hospitality Design* magazine, I stayed in the all-suites wing of the Mandalay Bay, the Delano, pronounced *de-LANE-oh* as if our thirty-second president had not existed, a situation I am sure would make Mr. Adelson happy. At the Delano all suites have separate rooms for living and sleeping, an extremely large bathroom, and a powder room just off the entry. In the hotel world, unless you have a powder room it is not a real suite. Enjoying this upgrade, I could not help thinking back on my brush with the law when I tried surreptitiously to slip into the pool at the Thunderbird.

I also recalled another experience involving gaming many years before. It was fortunate that I had visited Atlantic City in my youth, for memories of those flamboyant hotels, the Marlborough-Blenheim, the Traymore, and the like, were still in my mind when years later the most outlandish, flamboyant person in New York, Warner LeRoy, called and asked me to meet him in his vastly amusing gaudy apartment in the Dakota. Where else? He had a project in Atlantic City to redesign and expand the old Ritz-Carlton, which had fallen into disrepair. He intended to do the design himself but if I could come up with something extraordinary by Monday morning he would consider using me instead. I worked all weekend and produced a truly LeRoyish design, a fantasy hotel inspired by *The Wizard of Oz*. His father Mervyn LeRoy had directed that movie. Warner loved the design. The job was mine, the arches I had created were calculated, the five colors of mirror glass were chosen, everything approved, and most important the financing was in place, except that it wasn't. The financers turned out to be crooks, the Abscam scandal received headlines, and the project was canceled. No Ritz, no chance of instant fame as my design was innovative, forward-looking, and fun. Pick yourself up, brush yourself off, and start all over again.

CHAPTER 16

RENOVATIONS

Modest, Modern, or Very Louis XV

WHEN I WALK INTO LONDON'S RITZ Hotel today I am struck by the fact that it looks like it did when I first visited it in the 1950s. I wasn't there to stay, of course, since I had barely graduated from Exeter, but I'd commandeer Princess Margaret's corner table (we called it PM's) in The Ritz Restaurant where I'd meet my friends. We considered ourselves bright young things, reasonable facsimiles of the characters in Evelyn Waugh's *Vile Bodies*, as we happily had lunch and calmed down long enough to appreciate that wondrous gilded dining room. It is one of the most beautiful in the world, with marble columns, neoclassical statues, frescoes, a garland chandelier, and floor-to-ceiling windows look-

THE ASTOR COURT, ST. REGIS NEW YORK.

ing onto the garden and Green Park. Little in it has changed. Thank God (literally) that although the room has been freshened through the ages it has never been renovated, updated, or altered in any substantial way.

When the St. Regis reopened after a renovation in 1984 I gave Brooke Astor a tour of the Astor Court and King Cole Bar. I know she liked what she saw at the time, but I am quite certain she would not appreciate the changes the firm of Starwood made at the hotel in 2013. The single large chandelier of the court has been replaced by six small ones and the elegant paneled walls around Astor Court spattered with an incongruous mixture of paintings of various sizes that look like leftovers from the collection gracing the walls of Ralph Lauren's Polo Bar directly across Fifty-Fifth Street. Some imbibers in the King Cole Bar have to sit at high round tables, their feet floating above the floor, an experience available in any of the last remaining Irish bars on Third Avenue. What would Serge Obolensky and Salvador Dalí have said if they'd been forced to sit over drinks with their feet dangling in midair?

It is difficult to design a renovation of a historic hotel that allows the memory of its past famous guests to haunt the halls. I feel that the shiny redo of The Beverly Hills Hotel has pretty much banished the ghosts of Clark Gable and Carole Lombard. By the time I was asked to renovate the St. Regis in the 1980s, the ghosts had gone from there, too. Serge and Salvador had fled after seeing printed Hawaiian fabrics slapped on the walls of the bedrooms. New York had lost one of its great legendary hotels, temporarily at least.

The city was to lose many more permanently: the old Wal-

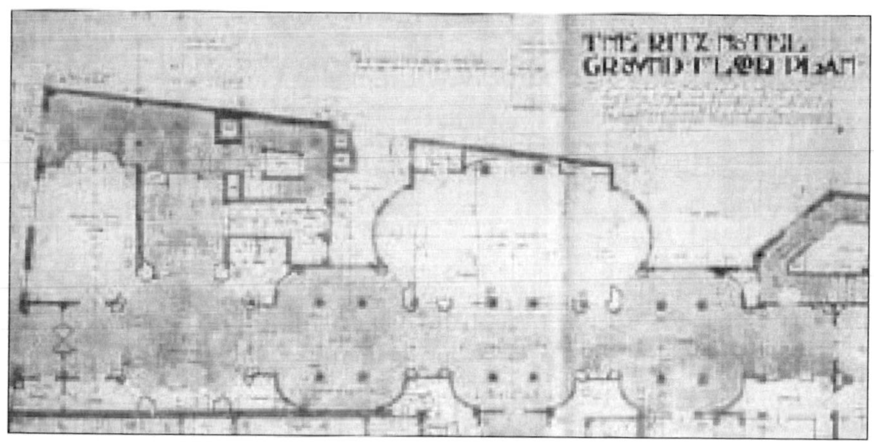

RITZ HOTEL, LONDON.

The lobby plan depicts a succession of public spaces.

dorf Astoria on Fifth Avenue and Thirty Fourth Street, the Ritz-Carlton, the Astor, and the Savoy Plaza on Fifth and Fifty-Ninth Street opposite Central Park (replaced by the General Motors Building). The Plaza has remained, of course, but it contained until recently over eight hundred rooms, too large for a true grand palace hotel. The Gotham was the right size, with a Gilded Age exterior, but Pierre Cardin redesigned the hotel in an art nouveau style reflecting Maxim's in Paris, which he owns. I didn't understand how that period inspired him to locate the bathtubs in the bedrooms. They have gone. Now the Gotham is a Peninsula hotel, in far better hands and appropriately redesigned, largely due to us.

When I designed the St. Regis I felt strongly that New York should have at least one hotel in the Ritz tradition. Certainly its exterior evokes the spirit of the great palace style. With this in mind, my aim was to make people who walked in think the place had remained just as it had always been, which was quite a challenge considering it is 95 percent new. The St. Regis was a major renovation, a virtual gut job. I could be found on Saturday mornings measuring the height of the chair rails in the Wrightsman Galleries for French Decorative Arts at the Metropolitan Museum. They are thirty inches high as a rule, not the thirty-six inches used by most designers these days. My aim was to give New York a hotel that recalled the great palaces of Europe and beyond.

ST. REGIS NEW YORK.

This plan shows the new configuration of the lobby with the Astor Court and King Cole Bar.

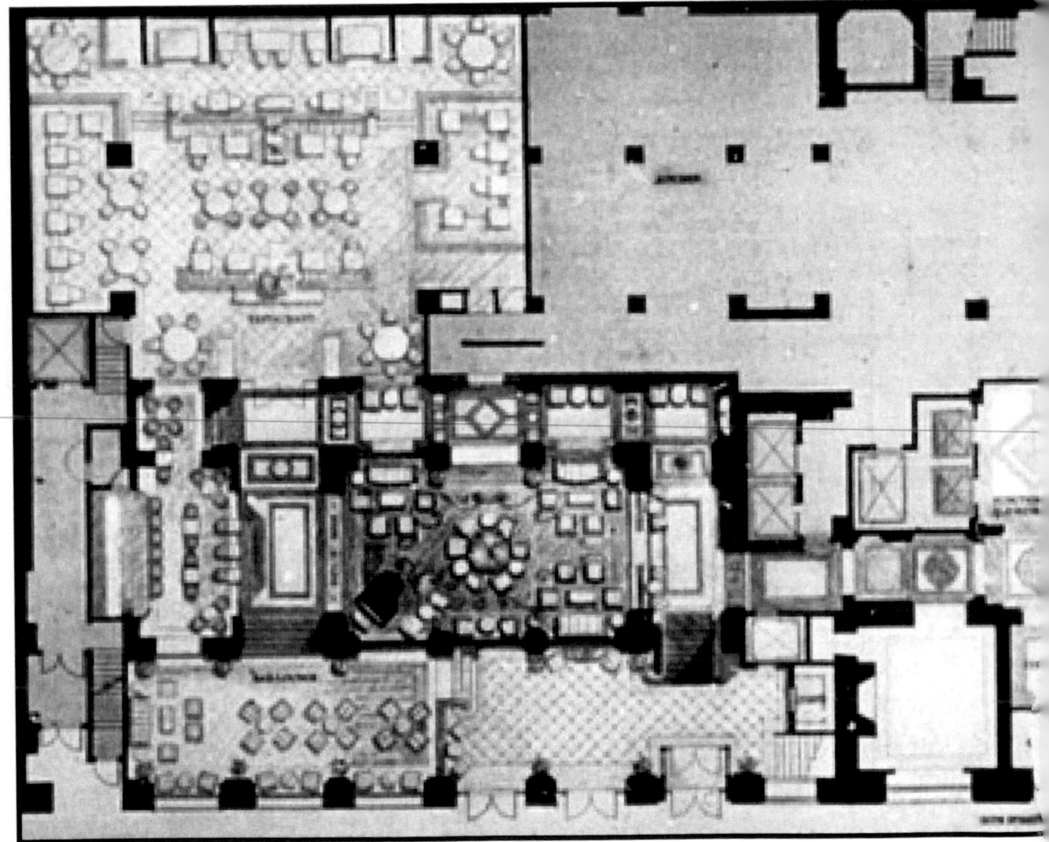

My decision to do a straight re-creation of a hotel as it looked from the time of its opening was out of step with the current style. Robert Venturi had designed an addition to the National Gallery in London using traditional materials such as limestone and bronze in nontraditional ways and slapping a couple of Corinthian pilasters onto the façade. In period rooms you needed to add a chair or two with a six-foot-high back to tell your guest that you were living in the 1990s, not during the turn of the century. But scorned as I may have been, the St. Regis was happily embraced by New Yorkers who were unaware that its public and guest rooms were anything but original. In this case, the seemingly effortless authenticity signaled a successful renovation, a job well done.

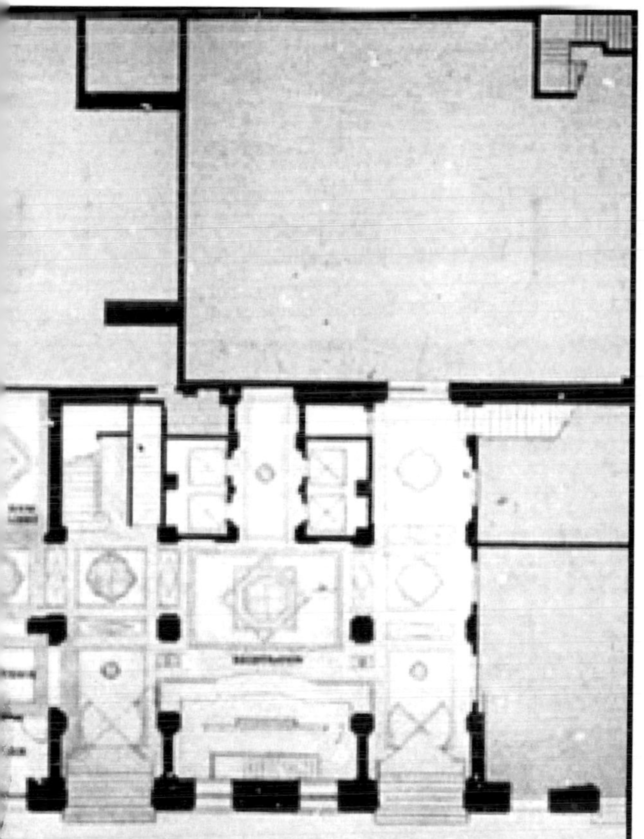

No matter what the style of a hotel's décor, whether simple, modern, or Louis XV classic, all its rooms and public spaces are freshened up every six or seven years to avoid looking tired and unloved. I have never found a decorator charged with re-covering furniture and repainting walls courageous enough to admit that the former designer had gotten it right and that a new scheme was not required. So do not fall in love with the look of your favorite room in your favorite hotel. It will not be the same on your next visit in a few years. And if you happened to admire a certain lobby, restaurant, or bar, odds are that it, too, will be altered. Wilson Associates from Dallas created a delightful, colorful plant-filled atrium for what used to be the charming, if modest, four-story Society Hill Sheraton Philadelphia. Since the opening, every new firm that has redesigned it has darkened the once cheerful lobby. I can no longer bear to go there even for a glass of wine, never mind if I am desperate for one after traipsing around historic, picturesque Society Hill.

Another type of renovation is in full swing in New York and indeed around the world: converting office buildings into apartments and hotels, some in our most iconic towers. The Woolworth Building and 70 Pine will become apartments, and so will others like the Crown Building on Fifth Avenue, the MetLife on Madison Square, and even the Sony Building, which was once Philip Johnson's AT&T Building. With the exception of the Woolworth Building, I have done schemes for them all, schemes that were never realized. It is fair to say that we have all had part of our youth misspent so I must confess that many years ago when the otherwise very responsible development firm of Tishman Speyer asked me to convert the Radio City Music Hall and the tower above into a hotel, the theater lobby into a hotel lobby, and the theater itself into a ballroom, I accepted the offer. Terrible idea, and thank God the project was abandoned. I have to admit, though, that the theater's incredible grand staircase and its incomparable art deco details would have put even the Waldorf Astoria's to shame. But I would have been disgraced. No future

Preservation League award for me. How could I have participated in the discussion of such a desecration? Marcel Breuer's first scheme for building a tower for Pan Am called for the destruction of Grand Central Station. At least our folly never went far enough to attract the attention of Mrs. Onassis.

The people who frequent newly renovated grand hotels may have the money but they certainly don't have the style of those who frequented the Ritz, the Plaza Athénée, The Gritti Palace, and indeed the St. Regis in days gone by, long gone by. It was always my aim to design spaces that complimented the guests, making them look as attractive as possible, and as if they belonged. When Albert Hinckey and I were responsible for the interior of a new riverboat, the *Mississippi Queen*, the job of interior designer had been given to someone from SOM who was schooled in a hard-line, strictly minimalist style not exactly compatible with the over-sixty-five, leisure-suit-sporting clients who would be clambering aboard in sneakers and flip-flops. We took over and designed the spaces more sympathetically, making them more detailed, more broken down, and more decorative in a contemporary way. Most important, we made these folk feel both comfortable and welcome.

I am not sure I know how to renovate grand historic hotels for today's guests, most of whom look to me to be extremely young and as if they would be uncomfortable wearing anything but jeans and an occasional jacket (not of the blue blazer kind), but never a tie. Such informality is fine and dandy except in an elaborately designed space such as The Peninsula Paris on the Avenue Kléber, which is all marble mirrors, chandeliers, and gilt everywhere. Everywhere!

ST. REGIS NEW YORK. *The Astor Court, looking toward the King Cole Bar (left) and from the lobby (below).*

The lobby of the Ritz in Madrid is grand, too, but slightly old-fashioned and not the least bit glitzy. During a recent visit I was struck by how the traditional fabrics, in hues of deep blue, rose, gold, and beige, flattered the crowd enjoying this lofty space. As virtually everyone was in jeans (except me, of course), I was able to see that the color of denim matched the blues of the fabrics in the lobby; the effect was quite harmonious. Of course the hotel is about to be renovated. This time Mandarin Oriental will be doing the job and I fear that they will emulate the colors used in the formerly grand Palace Hotel across the way. It's done up in bright colors and jazzy patterns and appointed with rather funky-looking furniture. The crowd in jeans looked dreadful: The faded blue against the bright fabrics made the people look shabby and a little unkempt.

By the way, occasionally I do wear jeans, but not in grand palace hotels. To celebrate her fiftieth birthday my daughter Elizabeth chose The Miami Beach Edition, a 1950s hotel that Ian Schrager recently renovated. He has turned the almost venerable but hardly memorable Seville into a truly delightful place. Forget the intricate moldings, gilt-framed mirrors, and lavish chandeliers of the Ritz in Madrid. Schrager's use of concrete, wood, simple white fabrics, and seemingly hundreds of plants creates a warm and welcoming environment, as comforting to me as that of any traditional grand hotel. Moreover, dear to my heart, the bathrooms contain only stall showers, no bathtubs. Mr. Schrager certainly understands hospitality, just as he did years ago when his staff allowed me and my lovely but conventionally dressed wife to pass by that infamous red velvet rope into Studio 54, and on numerous occasions at that. Formerly a Broadway house, the Fifty-Fourth Street Theater was transformed. Now, there was a renovation to remember!

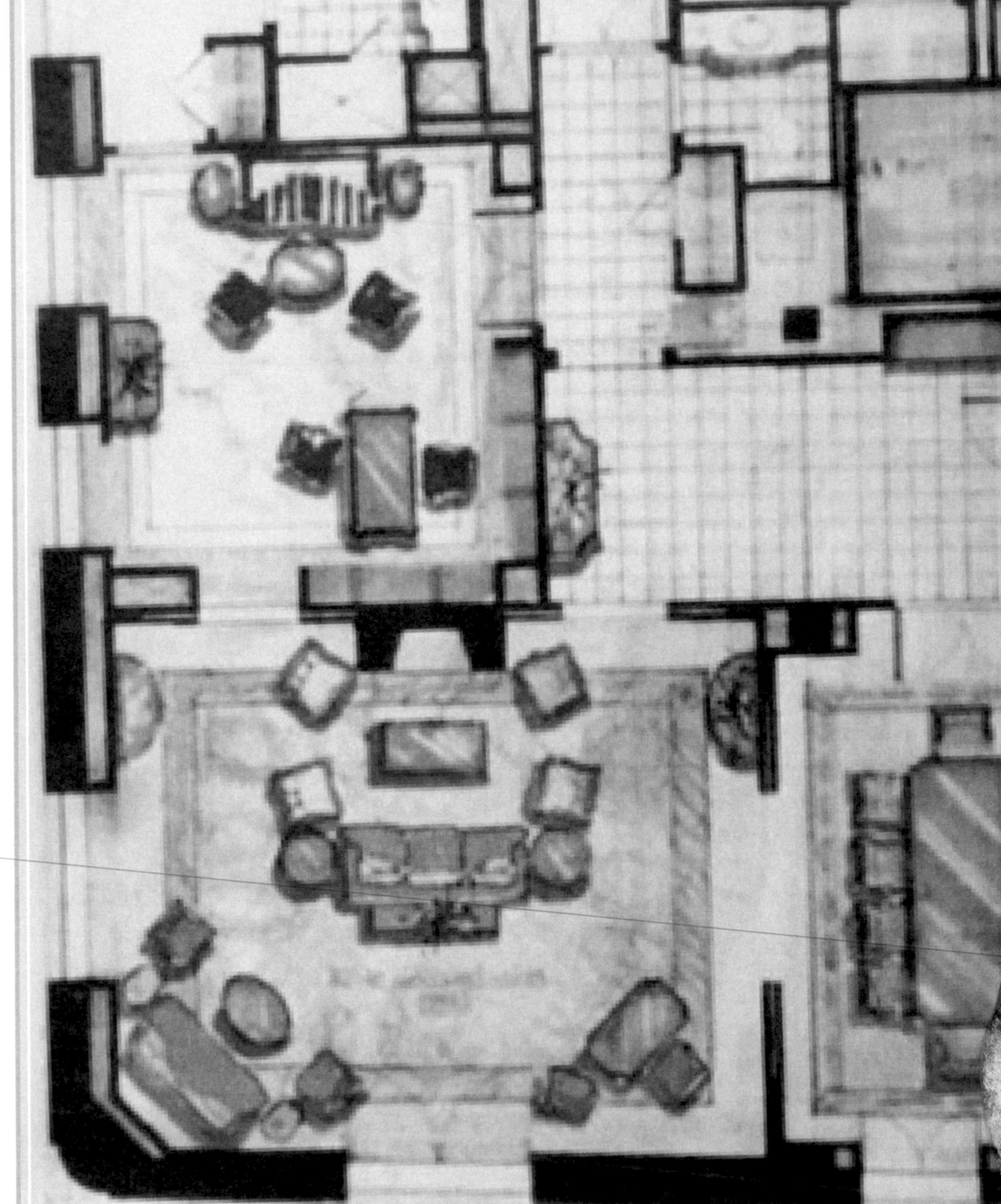

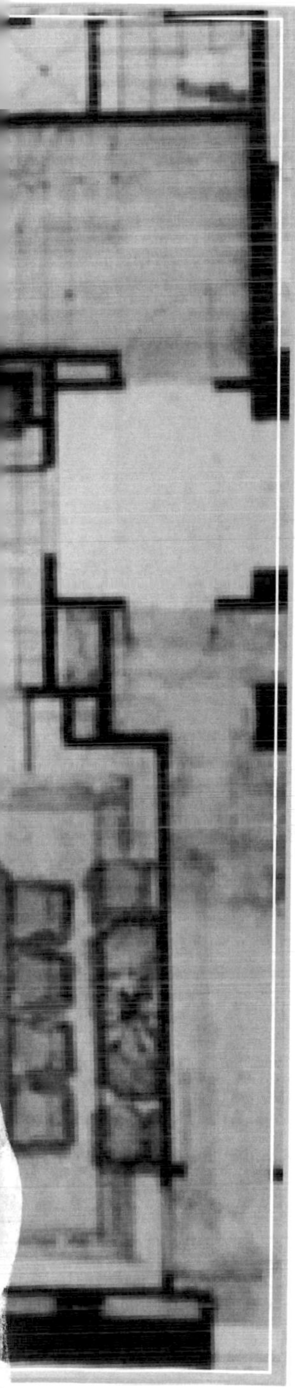

CHAPTER 17

HOTEL APARTMENTS

Convenience and a View

AS I HAVE SAID, AFTER THE WAR MANY affluent Greeks living in New York could not gain approval from stuffy co op boards to buy fancy apartments on Park and Fifth avenues, so being fancy themselves they chose to live in hotels, often in The Pierre, also on Fifth Avenue. Those apartments had one disadvantage: You had to travel through the hotel lobby to get to the elevators, the same elevators used by hotel guests. That could be awkward when you were sharing your trip with an overly exuberant partygoer leaving the hotel's popular grand ballroom below.

AUTHOR'S PARTIAL PLAN FOR WALDORF ASTORIA APARTMENT

Such an eventuality didn't seem to faze Vincent and Brooke Astor, or other apartment dwellers like William and Babe Paley, all of whom lived in the St. Regis and apparently didn't mind sharing the elevator with hotel guests. That hotel seems like an odd choice for New York's most elegant socialite and her media mogul husband.

The public elevator didn't seem to bother my friends who had apartments in the Carlyle, that bastion of understated elegance on the Upper East Side. After the war my family moved into a simple rental apartment around the corner from the Carlyle on Park Avenue. After her stay in the West Village my mother had claimed that she never wanted to live on Park Avenue, but there we were. I had my hair cut in the hotel's barbershop on the second floor; my dancing class at Mr. Benjamin's was held in its tiny ballroom, also on the second floor. Turn to the right, a haircut; turn to the left, a lesson on the Viennese turn, a fancy waltz step, under the watchful eye of Willie Durham.

Barely fourteen seems like an early age to learn how to turn the Viennese way, but boys who went to "the right schools" were immediately thrust into a world of early teen dances known as the Gets, the Mets, the Cols, and the Hols (the Get Togethers, the Metropolitans, the Colonys, and the Holidays, in case you possibly care). At that tender age I was far from breaking five feet and even farther from having a changed voice, so my parents wisely thought that to survive, I had better at least learn to dance well. I did dance well and did survive, which is why I took those dance lessons from Willie Durham on the second floor of the Carlyle Hotel across the hall from my barbershop.

Years later the hotel became important to me since my future in-laws lived there temporarily while their apartment on Fifth Avenue was being renovated. I took the Carlyle's public elevator to their apartments to ask Mr. Houghton for his daughter's hand, but the actual assent took place on the top of the Corning building in his not-small corner office. Meme Houghton, later Laura Beer, became a Phi Beta Scholar at Hunter School of Social Work and was an acknowledged humanitarian. She'd made a difference to a great many lives, as we learned at her memorial service at the Boat House where dozens of people spoke about how she had helped them with their problems. She was a remarkable human being, all the more so for putting up with me for sixteen years.

Hotel apartments in "mixed-use" projects are the most important element that affects developers' bottom line. The inclusion of a deluxe hotel adds to the prestige of the project and adds enormously to the value of the apartments. That explains why apartment buildings are built above the likes of the Four Seasons, Ritz-Carlton, St. Regis, and Mandarin Oriental and not above Holiday Inns and Embassy Suites, comfortable as those hotels may be. The latter are not deemed prestigious enough to increase the value of luxurious apartments. I think it's unfortunate that developers don't combine Holiday Inns with more modestly priced apartments. Such a project would offer the same conveniences afforded by high-end developments, such as shared maid service, restaurant deliveries, concierge use, spa and health club, maximum security, and very often a shopping center below.

Although my firm was the architect of the Mandarin Oriental, I see little advantage in living over a shopping center like the one at the Time Warner Center. Yes, some of the restaurants are

THE CARLYLE IN NEW YORK CITY.

This apartment is similar to the one where my in-laws lived temporarily.

superb, especially the astronomically priced Per Se (or so my daughter tells me). And my good friend Mel Blum, with whom I conceived several plans at Vornado Realty Trust, lived in an apartment above the Trump International Hotel across the street; nice man, bad choice of landlord. If Mel so desired he could take the elevator down to Jean-Georges, the restaurant below. For me having Pink, Bose, and Coach below me or next door does little to enhance the quality of my life no matter how glamorous my hotel apartment or fabulous the view.

Neither would having Hermès, Gucci, Louis Vuitton, and Chanel a few steps away add to my sense of well-being. My need for Hermès ties is nonexistent, as years ago I gave away my vast collection to be sold for charity, preferring the ties from Seigo on Upper Madison Avenue, which are far more stylish and original and are not worn by every doctor, lawyer, and chief in New York. I much prefer shopping on Lexington Avenue where you can find soups, sandwiches, salads, meat, fish, cheeses, flowers, cleaners, health foods, liquor, and drugs (the legal kind) within a couple of blocks from my front door. Not Per Se, but cozy and local, Lex Restaurant is around the corner and now filled with new friends who never darkened the door of Swifty's. While living above Chanel may be classy, living over Duane Reade is far superior from a convenience point of view. Having lived on Sixty-Sixth Street and Lexington where there were few local stores around, I have to admit that convenience is in many ways more important to me than luxurious living. A sudden need for Tylenol or dark chocolate is easily satisfied in three minutes and at all hours. Mixed-use living at its very best.

As I have gone on in a rather dispassionate way about hotel apartments you might not suspect that I lived in one for many months in 1959, in Athens no less. Hardly to be compared with the Grande Bretagne, or the King George catty-corner from my hotel on Syntagma Square, the New Angleterre Hotel was in a delightfully shabby turn-of-the-century building that exuded charm and coziness. My home was by itself on the top floor and was the only apartment in the hotel. Replete with a well-stocked English library and a blind maid who took wonderful care of me although she spoke only Greek, it cost me one dollar a night. For two weeks I had the distinct pleasure of spending a great deal of time with fellow guests, Beat poet Gregory Corso, a distant acquaintance from Harvard, and his friend and suddenly my new best friend, Tennessee Williams. On most days we had long lunches at a taverna around the corner from our hotel, and although they appeared to like me, they couldn't understand why I went back to work at an actual office after our long retsina-fueled lunches. After I left them they would take a bottle of scotch to a fisherman or two they might find hanging around the piers in Piraeus. They had a very different agenda for the remainder of their day and night from mine. I was just out of architectural school enjoying a new city with new friends, and making enough money to afford my own apartment high up in the New Angleterre. Hotel apartment living was at its best for me during that golden year. The historic building I loved so much was torn down to be replaced by an office block currently housing a McDonald's. No trace left of the romantic world I lived in during 1959. *Antio sas!*

CHAPTER 18

PACKING, TIPPING, AND OTHER MATTERS

SOME GUIDEBOOKS SUCH AS ROUGH Guides suggest that you stay only in simple hotels. Obviously that is essential advice for those on a strict budget, but for others I would suggest mixing up the choices without feeling guilty. It is a shame to miss the chance of a night in the Old World ambience of a grand palace hotel or the sybaritic pleasure of a stay at an exotic cottage where you can dip into your own private infinity pool (once again I admit that I've never treated myself to that ultimate indulgence).

The same advisers maintain that when you are traveling on land the best way to go is by train. In most cases I agree. But occasionally I hire a car and driver. I did this when Tyree and I

THE GRITTI PALACE IN VENICE.

visited the Vienna Woods, and on another occasion when we went for a stupendous lunch in the country miles outside of Strasbourg at l'Auberge de l'Ill. Driving our own car after a three-star meal and two bottles of wine would hardly have been prudent. For the most part, though, we eat at bistros and brasseries (does anyone know the difference between those two?), trattorias and tavernas, preferring the casual ambience and food. For the likes of us, L'Auberge with car and driver is rare indeed but much appreciated.

In Paris we occasionally screw up our courage and see if the powers that be will allow us to sit on the red banquettes beneath the oak-paneled walls of the main room at the first-rate but super-snobby Le Voltaire (no car and driver required to go there since it's on the Left Bank opposite the Louvre). No stars, either; it is not even in the Michelin Guide. Unlisted. When we were at the restaurant last year, securely placed on that red banquette in the back, I noticed Judy and Leonard Lauder sitting across the room. Leonard was enjoying my favorite first course there, the famously 99 percent of a euro ($1.12) *oeuf en gelée*, a wondrous single perfectly cooked egg. In case you think its price is indicative of the rest of your delicious meal at this charming and somewhat self-important restaurant, one look at your fellow diners will persuade you that you are not in your average bistro or brasserie. Unless you are as well known as your fellow diners, your jeans should have been left at home.

Whether you are going by airplane, boat, bus, train, or car, it is important to travel light. On my recent trip to California, I was reminded by my almost-niece Nina Houghton of a time when the Beers and the Houghtons traveled together, spending a week in the south of France and another at the Cipriani in Venice. Having learned from my aunt Ethel the necessity of traveling light, the members of our family packed one shoulder bag each containing all that was needed for their stay in a rented villa in Mougins and the super-fancy Cipriani. *Bravi* all, especially Meme!

At the train station at Nice, I took a picture of Maisie with my Instamatic camera, the iPhone of the 1970s, as she sat atop a pile of no less than ten T. Anthony suitcases. She was, of course, appropriately dressed for travel, her hair partly concealed by a white scarf. As the express pulled in, Jamie yelled at me to remain with the bags while he secured seats for us. The others dutifully boarded, leaving me to watch over the luggage, and watch I did as the train pulled out of the station, leaving me in possession of those ten pieces of T. Anthony luggage. Mercifully, in short order a local choo-choo painstakingly pulled in, and I managed with the help of two strangers to get the bags onto the train. Most of the seats in the compartment and the racks above were filled with their family's suitcases and bags. I can only imagine what the other passengers thought of me, alone with so much stuff, particularly on a local train. Nuts. *Nuts!*

At the Italian border we had to change trains, a challenge that triggered my handing out twenty-dollar bills to anyone willing to help. In Milan, another train, more money dispensed. Finally as night was falling, I arrived at the station in Venice where fortunately a Cipriani boat was waiting.

When I reached the hotel, I found the family happily ensconced, enjoying the sunset over the towers and dome of San Giorgio as they sipped their drinks on the sublime terrace. When he saw me, Jamie said, "We didn't go back because I knew you could handle it." His confidence was not misplaced. I did indeed handle it.

The virtues of traveling light are hardly controversial, but when it comes to how much to tip, answers are less clear. Tipping is a personal decision inevitably made alone, after a taxi ride, a meal out, or a stay in a hotel. Back in the day when I dined with women who were actually older, I usually picked up the bill. But a few grandes dames were still alive, and before they all expired to that great Southampton in the sky, I was occasionally treated by one such as Kay Meehan to a meal at Mortimer's (which later became Swifty's, in another location), where I would always order the least expensive item on the menu. My hostess nearly always pulled a tiny flashlight from her handbag and painstakingly doubled the tax instead of simply adding 20 percent to the bill.

My philosophy about tipping starts at home with the people around my apartment: the superintendent, doorman, handyman, those who make deliveries, and the barber down the block. Farther afield are the people who take care of me at the Knickerbocker and Metropolitan Opera clubs, The Century, and so on, and after that all the rest: the neediest, those good souls who deliver God's love, Planned Parenthood, ACLU, the two Mets, schools, and of course Armel, who gives me my usual table in the front room of La Grenouille. Once again, priorities.

Hotel tipping can be trickier. Certain things are a given. I hand at least three dollars to the man who brings up my bag, five dollars to the maid for the first night, ten for the second, and thereafter twenty for a long stay, maybe more at a fancy hotel. If a concierge is particularly helpful in changing my existing plane reservations, securing a seat far forward on the aisle, or procuring a decent ticket to a sold-out show in London I show my appreciation.

When leaving The Gritti Palace, I tip in the most excessive way starting with the then room manager, Nino, for giving me my favorite room on the floor facing west above the rooftops and chimneys, a room that is aglow at sunset. If Nino was gone and my usual room was not available: no tip. Next I give to the terrace captain, who secures the best tables by the Grand Canal for me and my party. And I also tip the maître d', the evening bartender, the sweet little bar boy, and finally the bellboys who load my bags into the motorboat for the airport.

In a different world, at The Standard, Hollywood, I have also received delightful service. But my tipping there has been nonexistent except for the maid, since so many different nice people take care of me.

Does anyone still practice a routine of elaborate tipping? I suspect the titans of industry do not. I imagine they assume that special service is their due, so they don't bother. Unfortunately, I want to be well served, and not only well served but also well loved. This can be a very expensive aspiration whether I'm taking a taxi, eating out, or staying in a hotel.

Some people like to make use of rewards programs. I do not turn my nose up at these savings offered to frequent customers. I punch in my telephone number when I'm buying toothpaste at Duane Reade or paper clips at Staples. On a grander scale, I fly almost exclusively on Delta to keep my gold status. I nearly always go business class to avoid long lines and check in with a real person, since I've never mastered those punch-in machines. I am not above availing myself of the amenities and free white wine in the lounges, either.

One of the most popular awards program in the hotel industry is Starwood's. I often end up at one of their properties, from my recent stay at Le Méridien Vienna back to the days when I was a regular at The Gritti Palace in Venice, which is part of their Luxury Collection brand. Somehow I never thought of The Gritti Palace in terms of rewards programs. Several years ago I booked three Gritti rooms for my granddaughter, Tyree, and me for five days over Easter, and when I checked out I signed the bill as I tend to do, not looking at it until I got home, not wanting to spoil the rest of the trip. In the process I neglected to take credit for our five-day stay in three rooms at full seasonal rates. Losing so many points has discouraged me from further participating in their program. Tyree registers religiously, so presumably he can take us back to The Gritti Palace, even though I expect his lifetime of rewards would cover no more than one night at that once intimate yet grand hotel.

My lesson on the importance of traveling light was not observed here.

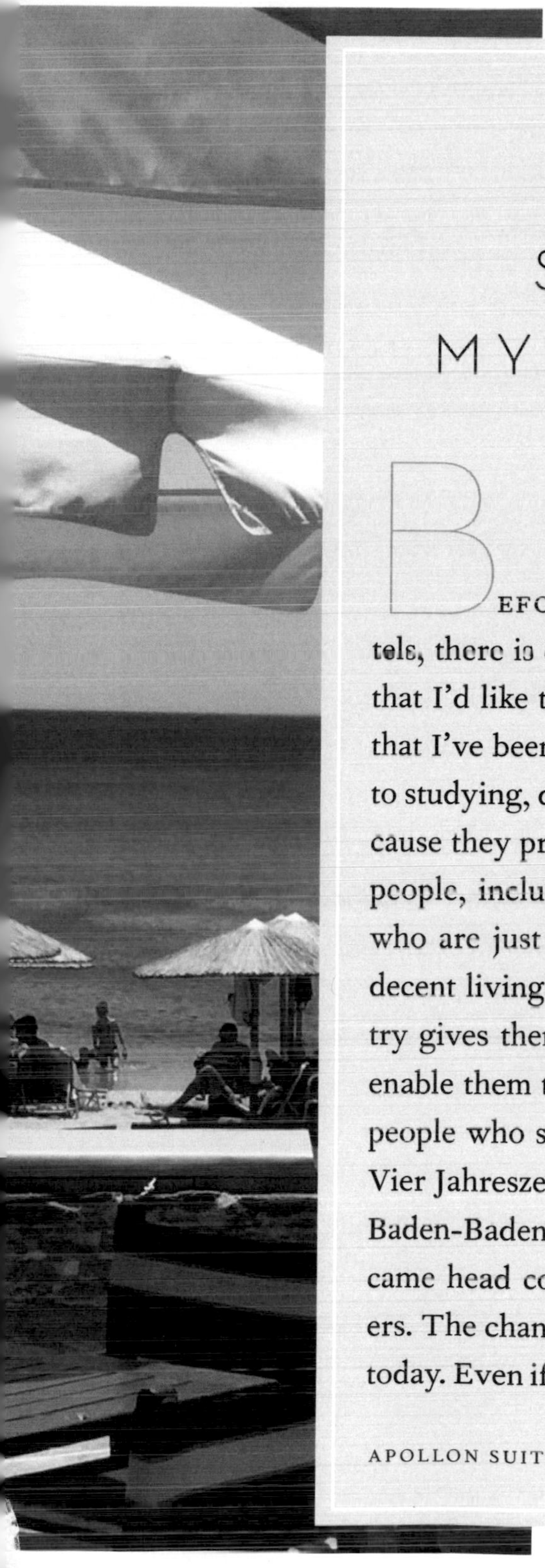

CHAPTER 19

SOME OF MY FAVORITES

BEFORE I DISCUSS MY FAVORITE HOtels, there is one side of the hospitality industry that I'd like to touch on. I am proud and happy that I've been able to devote so much of my life to studying, designing, and staying in hotels, because they provide work for many thousands of people, including millions of unskilled workers who are just starting out and hoping to earn a decent living. Even more important, this industry gives them a chance to learn skills that will enable them to advance. In years gone by many people who started as busboys or porters at the Vier Jahreszeiten in Hamburg, Brenners Park in Baden-Baden, and similar hotels eventually became head concierges, or even general managers. The chance for such advancement still exists today. Even if the goal is not to end up like one of

APOLLON SUITES HOTEL ON THE GREEK ISLAND EVIA.

those haughty head concierges who have intimidated me at The Gritti Palace in Venice and Plaza Athénée in Paris, there are many aspects of the hotel business to learn—housekeeping, food preparation, front-desk and banquet managing, accounting, engineering, and on and on. The hospitality industry is, in its own way, very democratic, always ready to reward good work with advancement to the very top. It reflects the values I was brought up to believe in.

Now that I have devoted most of my creative life to designing hotels, the question I am asked most often is, "Which one is your favorite?" Thirty years ago I might have answered with Brenners Park-Hotel or The Gritti Palace. I often spent Christmas at the former. Germany does that holiday so well, with festive markets in the squares, warm glühwein, and lavishly decorated Tannenbaums. I usually went with Tyree and a grandchild or two and once with my brother- and sister-in-law, Jamie and Maisie Houghton. I was by then divorced from Jamie's sister, but the three of us remained close friends. I had alerted the hotel that quality was coming. Aside from everything else, Jamie's grandfather had been our ambassador to Berlin in the 1920s. Mr. Houghton and his sister Elinor Cole remembered the hotel fondly, having spent several summers there. The information was duly noted to the management. Given this background the Houghtons were extremely excited about visiting Baden-Baden and staying at the renowned Brenners Park-Hotel.

After my introduction you would have expected them to receive a particularly warm welcome, along with flowers and even champagne in their room. Instead they were greeted coldly, with a haughtiness only that kind of hotel can exhibit when you are not "known." They were given an inferior room looking at the driveway in front of the building, not over the garden and the River Oos in the back. As I think of it now, the only explanation I can give is that they had driven up in a modest rented Ford, the likes of which had never been seen in this Mercedes-dominated Black Forest part of the world. I have never returned to Brenners Park-Hotel.

At The Gritti Palace I have always occupied the same room, not with a view of the Grand Canal but looking over romantic rooftops facing west toward the sunset. Some years ago Tyree and I brought my granddaughter Nuala to Venice. I fantasized about hiring a water taxi from the railroad station that would take us to the hotel all the way up the Grand Canal without using the shortcut that saves lira but lessens the drama. As we passed Larry Lovett's lovely palazzo on the left, just before the Rialto Bridge, he would be on his terrace waving a welcome. Then we'd travel under the Accademia Bridge and over to the dock in front of the formidable Gritti Palace where my friends among the staff would "welcome back Mr. Beer." They'd lead us to that most ravishing of all terraces, filled with the usuals sitting under the blue and white awning and straining their heads to see who was arriving next. Such a lovely vision. Unfortunately it was shattered on that occasion. The hotel's terrace was under construction, and unusable. The Gritti without its terrace is like the Cipriani without its pool. Worse, my beloved room had been given to another. Two favorite hotels, two disappointments. I would have to look elsewhere for a favorite.

I cannot claim that The Peninsula Shanghai is my ultimate favorite. But aesthetically it's the most successful hotel that I have both designed and seen built. Many of my other proposals through the years were more adventurous and forward-looking, but alas, they were never realized. The Peninsula is extremely popular, especially with those who used to be called part of "the carriage trade." My friends, many of whom fit easily into that category, tell me that they wouldn't dream of staying anywhere else (a compliment somewhat to be discounted as they are, after all, my friends). On the Bund there are two other grand hotels once in disrepair that have been renovated very successfully, the Fairmont Peace Hotel and the Waldorf Astoria Shanghai. In the case of the Peninsula, the design is original, built from the ground up.

I am proud of my accomplishment at The Peninsula Shanghai and happy to visit that hotel. However, I always stay at the old Four Seasons and not the shiny new one across the river in dreaded Pudong. This hotel is an easy walk to the city center, where People's Square, the Shanghai Museum, and the Grand Theatre are located. The museum has a comprehensive Chinese collection, and its early bronzes are worth crossing the Pacific to see. As for the theater, its vast interior is well laid out, and I have attended many kinds of performance there, ranging from the Cologne Opera's presentation of Wagner's *Ring Cycle* to *Mamma Mia!*

The Four Seasons is located in what city planners describe as a mixed-use area, consisting of not only office buildings and hotels but also upscale apartments, houses, affordable local shops, and restaurants, including one of my favorite neighborhood bistros in the world, Nova, which is French despite its name and has a lovely terrace facing a small park. A short walk away is the magical French Concession district with its historic buildings, the other reason for crossing the Pacific. The best time to come here is when the plane trees are in leaf and it is warm enough (although not too warm) to sit outside in one of the numerous gardens or rooftop restaurants.

Although I have not seen the renovated Four Seasons, the hotel will always remain special to me because of the service, which is, as far as I have experienced, the best in China: warm, caring, and professional. I can't say that all service in that country could be characterized that way. China may eventually outpace us economically but it will be a very long time before Mandarin replaces English as the world's universal language, and until it does it would behoove the front-desk staff at five-star hotels to learn English. The front-desk staff at The St. Regis Beijing, a well-located and lovely if conservatively designed hotel, is singularly lacking in that professionalism. On one occasion, in 2010, after I'd explained my past history with the St. Regis (including the fact that I'd designed the very hotel that had started the brand), I asked the young man behind the front desk if he would upgrade me to a small, modest suite. His mysterious answer was that this particular St. Regis did not have any suites. That would certainly have been news for President Obama, who was due to stay there while attending the APEC conference in the spring. Lost in translation.

If I were to pick the most awe-inspiring night I have ever spent it would not be one in a hotel room or even someone's house. I would have to choose the night I spent in a cell as a guest of the good monks who inhabit the Simonopetra Monastery on Mount Athos, which is built on a single huge rock over the tip of

SIMONOPETRA MONASTERY, MOUNT ATHOS, GREECE.

A virtual hotel for intrepid travelers—men only.

one of the peninsulas that jets out into the sea. The cell itself I do not remember, but I have never forgotten the cocktail hour when

I was served local wine on a terrace overlooking the magnificent row of balconies crowding the top of the ancient structure that rises over the shimmering sea far below. The monastery remains one of the most ravishingly beautiful pieces of architecture ever conceived, and for me to have sat there looking at the buildings on each side and the darkening Aegean beyond remains a cherished memory—all the more since the monks' hospitality extended to a delightful dinner of baby lamb, lemon-roasted potatoes, and a hearty red wine served in a candlelit chamber. The monastery has the most beautiful view ever, not to mention delicious food and wine, all free of cost. Now, *that* is hospitality! However, you have to be a man to enjoy it. No women allowed on the sacred mountain.

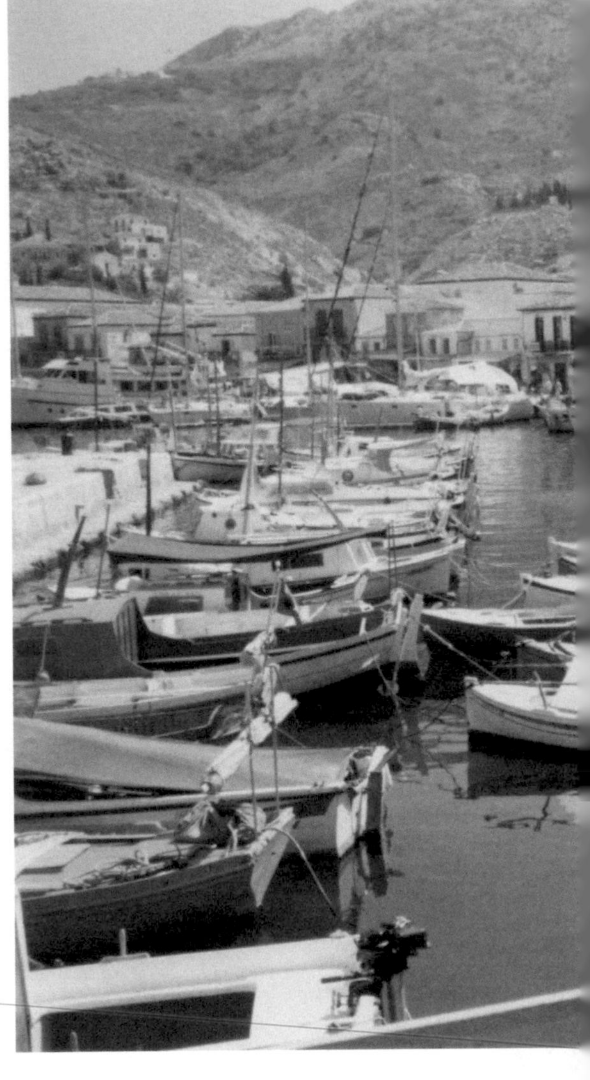

The hotel I most look forward to revisiting is not by the South China Sea; it faces the Aegean. Of all the hotels I have discussed in any detail, Apollon Suites on the Greek island of Evia is the simplest. It doesn't boast the classic lofty lobby or tree-shaded gardens of the Ritz in Madrid, or a monumental if imperfectly designed grand staircase like that of the Imperial in Vienna, and certainly not a garland restaurant on the order of the Ritz's in London. It has, however, a view not dissimilar to the one I enjoyed high up on the side of the monastery of Simonopetra in Mount Athos. It's not as spectacular, of course, but from my balcony on the top of the Apollon Suites' six-story tower I can look across to the Aegean all the way to the islands of Zea and Aegina.

Evia is happily one of the Greek islands least visited by foreign tourists, even though it's a scant hour by slow boat from Athens to a port town near Karystos. It's not a cutesy, Cycladic white village like those that were so wonderful to visit in the

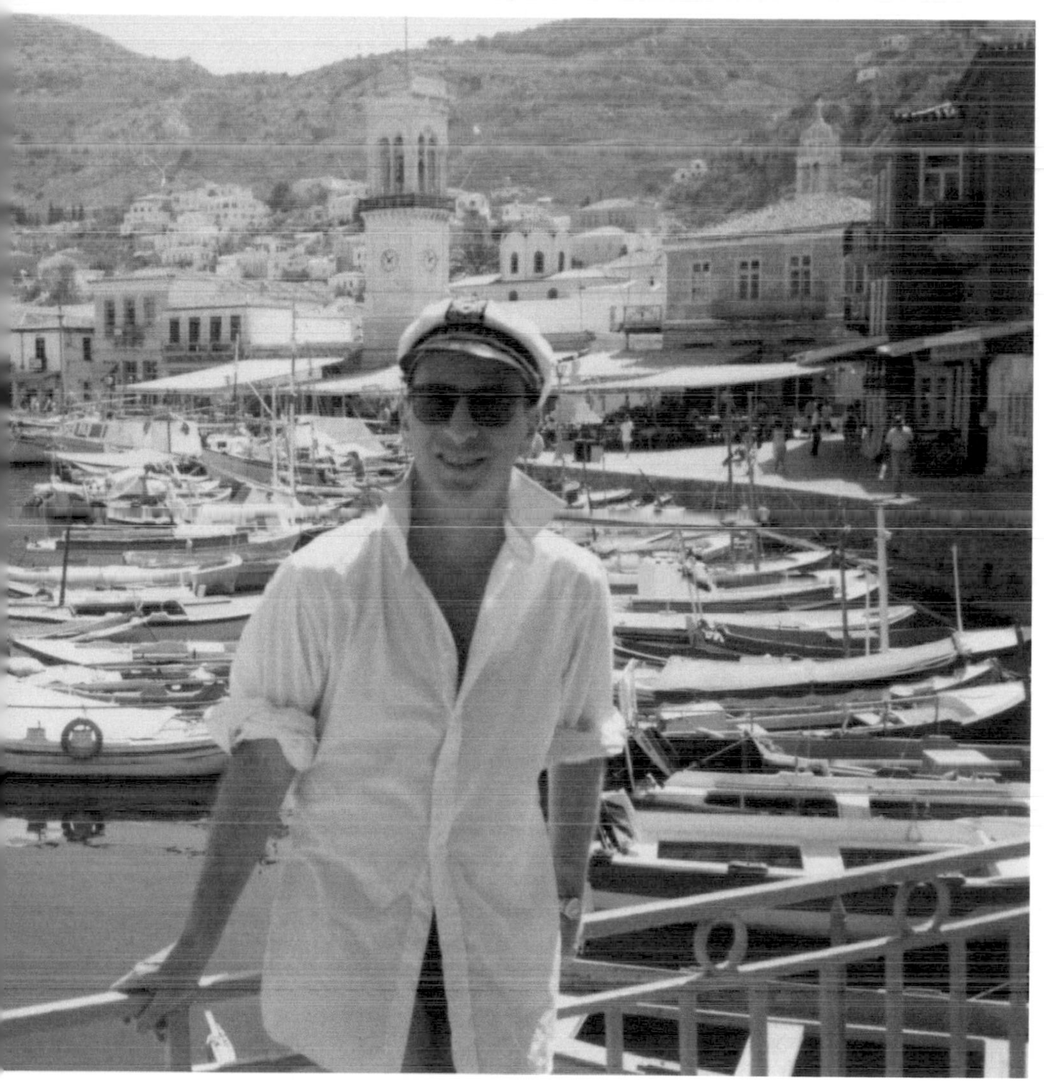

HYDRA, GREECE, 1959.

Happy, happy, with no grand hotels in sight.

1960s, nor is it overrun by hard-partying tourists or cruise ship refugees. There is one postcard stand in the only convenience store. The row of restaurants facing the port where few fishing boats are moored is typical of all the islands but hardly as charming as those in Hydra. Nothing special to attract foreigners. They are virtually nonexistent. Perfect.

When you enter the hotel you pass a small front desk and walk on flagstones directly out to the terrace, no glass impeding you. From the terrace there is a view of the beach and the hills on either side of the bay, opening to the sea with islands on the horizon. A classic Greek island view. The hotel itself is far from picturesque. It's a high-rise with an outside corridor leading to all-sea-facing rooms, painted white with minimal furniture and zero décor; very basic. In Greece the best way to enjoy the sun, sea, and air is in the simplest surroundings. Spare me the heavy lined silk curtains and plush armchair pillows of the Hotel Grand Bretagne. Today they belong on the Ringstrasse in Vienna. In Athens's Syntagma Square, even the royal palace is simple.

Upon my return to Karystos I will walk a short distance up the street and have lunch in a tavern by the sea, with the food served across a mostly deserted road. The view from about fifty feet above the beach out to sea is nearly beyond comparison. I will be sure to go on a weekday since the hotel is overrun by Greek families over the weekend; peace shattered. Families are fine as long as the children are your own. Since I've brought my family there twice, I can attest to that.

Sitting at this restaurant, listening to the crickets and gazing out to the sea past the tip of Attica to the islands, eating my tomato salad with olives and feta cheese, along with a small fish, *karpouzi* (watermelon), and some chilled Greek wine: This adds up to a fine place for me to contemplate the happy life I've led discovering and staying in hotels all over the world.

I WILL ALWAYS REMEMBER those first lunches with my parents in the old Sherry-Netherland bar, the infinitely more serious lunches with them at The Ritz Restaurant in London, swimming at the edge of but not *in* the Nile at the Winter Palace in Luxor, descending the curved staircase at the Shah Abbas in Isfahan, festive lunches on the terrace at the Hotel Des Bains, standing at the bar at the top of the Peninsula and gazing at the floodlit buildings on the Bund, knowing that my creation was part of that particular majestic ensemble.

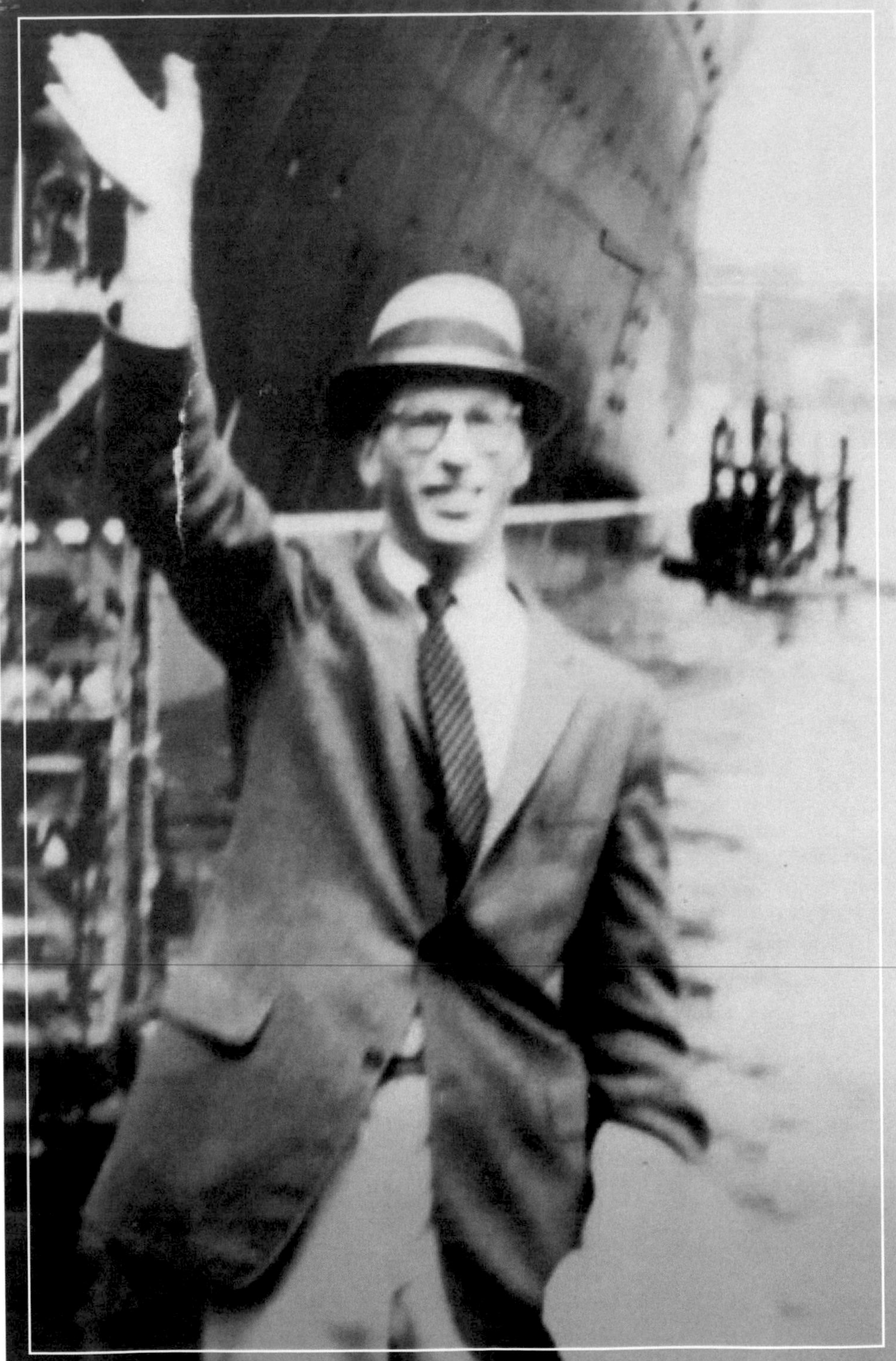

CHAPTER 20

THE GOLDEN AGE OF TRAVEL

When the World Was Mine

I'M ALWAYS READING ABOUT THE GREAT AGE of travel that took place during the eighteenth and nineteenth centuries when young men—yes, mostly men—from England and America were sent to the Continent to see the treasures of Rome, Florence, and Venice, and to visit other centers of art and culture. I would like to think that I was born at the right moment to enjoy another great and very special age of travel, the 1950s, very soon after the war, when I was a young man. The year I first went to the Continent was 1951.

At that time "getting there is half the fun"

THE AUTHOR BOARDING CUNARD'S SS *PARTHIA*, 1951.

held true if you were traveling first class on the great ocean liners such as the *Queen Mary*, the *Queen Elizabeth*, the *France*, or even the ill-fated *Andrea Doria*. But it was time-consuming and relatively expensive. You did not go to London for a long weekend. By airplane, it took twenty hours and two stops to get there.

The relative lack of fellow travelers allowed me the blessed solitude and time to fantasize that I was discovering new worlds. I was the only guest in the only possible hotel inside the walls of the medina in Marrakech. I was the one outsider enjoying the vast panorama of the great main square, the Jemaa el-Fna, watching merchants haggling with merchants, not with tourists, and marveling at the snakes preening and hissing for one another's amusement, since there were no bystanders around to be charmed by them. A few tourists might eventually appear after the midday sun, straggling over from the grand Mamounia hotel that was nearby but outside the Medina wall and, if you can believe it, as yet unknown to me so I never cruised it. By midday I was on my way to Fez by public bus, seeking a new solitary encounter with that as-yet-undiscovered city.

It was July when I visited Morocco, which partly explained the lack of tourists. It was equally hot in Santorini. Very hot indeed, as I walked one day along a dusty path over some hills down to the beach from the village, which is dramatically perched above the Aegean as the entire world now knows. Not then, apparently, since I was the only soul on the beach, alone, free, suitless, looking over the very spot where condos, hotels, and an airport would soon be constructed. To put it mildly, it was a unique experience to be savored forever.

I was in Egypt in Luxor when there were only two hotels. The Hotel Luxor was clean and respectable but hardly comparable with the legendary Winter Palace, which even then evoked the days long gone by that had seen hordes of Brits lounging on the terrace, escaping the London fog. It was my luck to have viewed the Nile when it was flooded, surrounding the great temples with endless lakes dotted with soaring palms. The Aswan Dam ended that dreamscape along with seven chain hotels built in Luxor. Those seasonal British families are most certainly wintering elsewhere.

In Greece, as late as 1959 you could walk up to the Acropolis through the Propylaea to watch the light reflected off the Parthenon at sunset. There was not a gate or even a fence to discourage you. To be almost alone watching the sun fall into the Aegean, with the Temple of Athena behind you, was magical. I did not bother to wear a bathing suit in Greece, since I was the lone person on the beach in Santorini, where there are now dozens of condos, many hotels, and the island's airport. I was also virtually alone inspecting the weathered beauty of the walls of the palaces and churches in Prague in the winter of 1990. The only tour buses in front of the great cathedral in Sofia were from the other Soviet bloc countries whose inhabitants would travel long distances to hear the immense choir and organ perform a great mass in the central cathedral, a surprising event in the most communist of communist countries. Of curious types like me there were none.

Of course I would love to go back to Rome and see the Caravaggios and Berninis at perhaps my favorite museum, the Borghese Gallery, only now you have to book your visit at least two days in advance, and even then you may be allotted a markedly inconvenient time slot.

In Paris, well before the Louvre Pyramid was built, you could line up with a few other art lovers in a covered arcade in a corner of the courtyard shielded from the weather. No rain, no crowds, no hassle, and no lines outside or in. Once the world was mine to explore almost alone, accompanied by my wheel-less suitcase, and enjoying what now I consider to have been the golden age of travel.

All in all, a life well led in the wonderful world of hotels.

ACKNOWLEDGMENTS

MY WONDERFUL PARENTS GAVE ME A SUPERB EDucation at Collegiate, Exeter, and Harvard, but I never learned to type. In those days Katharine Gibbs's secretarial school was not for boys. My nearly illegible scribbles on lined paper were transcribed first by the ever-faithful Maureen Abano and now by my current savior Dodie Draher. My ability to use my computer at all is thanks to Kristopher Monroe, who is in charge of dragging me into the twenty-first century in general and sorting my photos electronically for this book in particular. My editor Moira Hodgson tactfully removed some of my more flagrant name-drops and encouraged me by saying, "You have a voice." Who knew? My most heartfelt thanks to Maggie Simmons, who orchestrated this production, introducing me to book designer Barbara Bachman and photo editor Laurie Platt Winfrey of Carousel Research, who have given visual life to my memories. Thanks, too, to copy editor Laura Jorstad who was vigilant in keeping the smallest errors in grammar and facts from slipping by. Again, Maggie, and her friend and my cousin John Loengard, who accompanied me on my first trip to Italy in 1951, kept assuring me that one day this book would be ready for family and friends as well as those who share my passion for hotels simple and splendid.

PHOTO CREDITS

THE EDITORS ARE GRATEFUL FOR THE GENEROUS cooperation of all the hotels whose images are shown in this book, particularly The Ritz London for the cover photograph. Architectural drawings and personal images are from the author's archives; other photographs are noted below. Any errors or omissions are inadvertent and will be corrected in future editions.

ALAMY: Contents, Chronicle; pp. x–xi, Imagedoc; p. xviii (right), Neil Setchfield; p. 8, Zoonar; pp. 14–15, Brian Anthony; p. 28, AAWorld Travel; pp. 38–39, Bill Blackmann; pp. 44–45, Steve Vidler; p. 49, Premium Stock; pp. 74–75, Marmaduke St. John; p. 76, Advertising Archives; p. 80, Laurens Smak; p. 100, Travel Collection; pp. 118–119, Margaret S; pp. 142–143, Adam Eastland; pp. 146–147, Craig Lovell; p. 179, JLBvdWolf.

BBG-BBGM, pp. 12–13.

Melwyn Cobb, p. 87.

Courtesy Fran Parente, p. 42.

John Portman & Associates, pp. 34–35.

Courtesy Paul Warchol Photography, pp. 46–47.

Getty Images, Tom Stoddart Archives, pp. 70–71.

Thodoris Lakiotis 2006, pp. 186–187.

Shanghai Diary, p. 13.

Picture research by Laurie Platt Winfrey, Carousel Research

ABOUT THE AUTHOR

DAVID W. BEER, FAIA, is a native New Yorker who has spent most of his adult life on his beloved Lexington Avenue, first with his wife and two children on Sixty-Sixth Street and now a little farther uptown on Ninetieth Street, where he lives with his partner, Tyree Giroux. He was educated at Harvard College and the Harvard Graduate School of Design before embarking on his long and distinguished architectural career.

Beer became director of design in the New York office of Welton Becket, a large international firm specializing in the design of hotels. In 1984 he founded his own firm, BBG-BBGM, with two former partners from Becket. Soon his expertise was much in demand and he was sent to design projects all over the world, including Iran, Russia, Congo, Indonesia, and China. These trips reinforced his lifetime love of travel—instilled at an early age by his adventurous aunt Ethel, who took Beer on his first trip to Europe in 1951.